Where are the Resources for Lifelong Learning?

OECD
ORGANISATION FOR ECONOMIC CO-OPERATION AND DEVELOPMENT

ORGANISATION FOR ECONOMIC CO-OPERATION AND DEVELOPMENT

Pursuant to Article 1 of the Convention signed in Paris on 14th December 1960, and which came into force on 30th September 1961, the Organisation for Economic Co-operation and Development (OECD) shall promote policies designed:

- to achieve the highest sustainable economic growth and employment and a rising standard of living in Member countries, while maintaining financial stability, and thus to contribute to the development of the world economy;
- to contribute to sound economic expansion in Member as well as non-member countries in the process of economic development; and
- to contribute to the expansion of world trade on a multilateral, non-discriminatory basis in accordance with international obligations.

The original Member countries of the OECD are Austria, Belgium, Canada, Denmark, France, Germany, Greece, Iceland, Ireland, Italy, Luxembourg, the Netherlands, Norway, Portugal, Spain, Sweden, Switzerland, Turkey, the United Kingdom and the United States. The following countries became Members subsequently through accession at the dates indicated hereafter: Japan (28th April 1964), Finland (28th January 1969), Australia (7th June 1971), New Zealand (29th May 1973), Mexico (18th May 1994), the Czech Republic (21st December 1995), Hungary (7th May 1996), Poland (22nd November 1996) and Korea (12th December 1996). The Commission of the European Communities takes part in the work of the OECD (Article 13 of the OECD Convention).

Publié en français sous le titre :
COMMENT FINANCER L'APPRENTISSAGE À VIE

© OECD 2000
Permission to reproduce a portion of this work for non-commercial purposes or classroom use should be obtained through the Centre français d'exploitation du droit de copie (CFC), 20, rue des Grands-Augustins, 75006 Paris, France, Tel. (33-1) 44 07 47 70, Fax (33-1) 46 34 67 19, for every country except the United States. In the United States permission should be obtained through the Copyright Clearance Center, Customer Service, (508)750-8400, 222 Rosewood Drive, Danvers, MA 01923 USA, or CCC Online: *http://www.copyright.com/*. All other applications for permission to reproduce or translate all or part of this book should be made to OECD Publications, 2, rue André-Pascal, 75775 Paris Cedex 16, France.

Foreword

When they met in January 1996, OECD Education Ministers acknowledged the economic and social benefits from lifelong learning, and emphasised the importance of finding ways to pay for it.

In order to develop and reinforce strategies for achieving this goal, the Education Committee agreed to undertake three components of work: *i)* to survey the lifelong learning goals that Member countries have established, and identify the strategies they are pursuing to mobilise the investment in lifelong learning, and improve its returns and reduce its costs; *ii)* to examine in depth financing issues that arise in selected sectors of lifelong learning, and explore promising approaches to addressing the issues; and *iii)* to prepare a policy report that would provide a basis for an in-depth discussion by public authorities and the social partners, on what actions are needed to improve the affordability of lifelong learning.

This report was prepared under the first component of the OECD's activity on alternative approaches to financing lifelong learning. It was drafted by Professor Andy Green, Dr. Ann Hodgson, and Professor Gareth Williams of the Institute of Education, University of London; parts of the text were further elaborated by Gregory Wurzburg of the OECD Secretariat. It is based on country reports that provide a first glimpse of how selected OECD Member countries were addressing the challenge of finding the resources to implement strategies for lifelong learning for all. Experts from ten countries submitted reports. The countries are: Austria, the Czech Republic, Finland, Hungary, Italy, Japan, Korea, the Netherlands, Norway, and Sweden. In addition, the Secretariat, at the request of the Danish authorities, prepared a "capsule summary" of the situation in Denmark with regard to the issue of resources for lifelong learning. The text of the individual country reports can be found at the OECD web site for financing lifelong learning (*http://www.oecd.org/els/edu/*).

This report is published on the responsibility of the Secretary-General of the OECD.

© OECD 2000

Table of Contents

Introduction 7

Chapter 1. **Goals, Objectives, and Priorities** 9

    From advocacy to action 9
    Stages of formulating and implementing policy for lifelong learning 10
    Overview of the country goals for lifelong learning 11
    From policy goals to operational objectives 17
    Lifelong learning gaps and participation targets for closing them: evaluating
        different scenarios 21
    Expenditure gaps 27
    Conclusions 30

Chapter 2. **Increasing the Cost-effectiveness, Quality and Benefits of Lifelong
        Learning Opportunities** 33

    Introduction 33
    Difficulties in addressing cost-effectiveness and quality 33
    Strategies to improve cost-effectiveness and quality in initial education
        and training 35
    Tertiary education 44
    Other measures to improve the quality of lifelong learning opportunities . 49
    Equity issues 56
    Conclusions 59

Chapter 3. **Mobilising Financial Resources for Lifelong Learning** 61

    Introduction 61
    Secondary education and initial training: principal issues 63
    Tertiary education 80
    Adult participation in lifelong learning 92
    Conclusions 104

Chapter 4. **What Next?** 107

    The issue of affordability............ 107
    How ambitious a goal have countries set, and how costly will it be to achieve? 108
    Strengthening incentives to invest in lifelong learning: how can efficiency
        and cost-effectiveness be improved, and benefits increased? 109
    Putting incentives to work: how can financial resources be mobilised?............ 111
    From marginal change to paradigm shift............ 112

Bibliography 115

    Annex 1.   Estimating Lifelong Learning Gaps 117
    Annex 2.   Estimates of Participation Gaps............ 119
    Annex 3.   Estimated Costs of Closing Participation Gaps............ 127

Introduction

At the meeting of the Education Committee at Ministerial Level, 16-17 January 1996, Education Ministers recognised the economic and social benefits from lifelong learning, and emphasised the importance of finding ways to pay for it. Ministers observed in their communiqué:

"There are substantial potential benefits from lifelong learning, and increased investment is likely to be needed if these are to be realised. Incentives must be found which will mobilise new resources, but how the responsibility for such investments is shared will depend on the traditions and circumstances of different Member states. While some countries are prepared to fund lifelong learning largely from the public purse, others will need to find ways of mobilising new investment if lifelong learning is to be affordable (…). Ministers (…) request the OECD to deepen its analysis of policies which offer incentives for learners, their families, employers and other partners to mobilise larger investments for learning and which promote cost-effectiveness, equity and quality."

The goal of achieving lifelong learning for all is being pursued at a time of severe constraints on resources. Public authorities are under intense political pressure to limit spending; enterprises are under intense competitive pressure to reduce costs or otherwise ensure that investments are cost-effective and improve productivity; individuals are constrained by a combination of slow real wage growth, and high and persistent risk of unemployment.

The extent to which lifelong learning for all can be made a reality depends in large degree on the extent to which lifelong learning can be made more "affordable". This in turn depends on three issues:

– What is meant by "lifelong learning" and how ambitious or how modest is the vision of lifelong learning to be implemented.

– Whether lifelong learning can deliver greater value for money, thus strengthening the economic and social incentives to invest in lifelong learning.

– Whether net new financial resources can be found in the public and private sector, possibly by making it easier to pay out of past savings or future benefits.

© OECD 2000

This report synthesises evidence and views presented in eleven country reports regarding these three issues. Chapter 1 provides an overview of the progress in countries towards specifying what is meant by lifelong learning for all, and what its implementation implies. Chapter 2 reviews the situation and developments that impinge on rate of return to lifelong learning, the strength of the incentive for various actors to invest in lifelong learning. Chapter 3 considers the means by which various actors pay for lifelong learning, the extent to which those means interact with the incentives to improve value for money, and the possibility of finding net new financial resources. Chapter 4 draws summary conclusions and identifies unresolved issues.

Notwithstanding the political commitment in OECD Member countries to implement strategies for lifelong learning, countries differ from one another with respect to their starting point, priorities, the pace of progress and the availability of information for evaluating such progress. This complicates the task of presenting a comparative and timely picture of developments. The reader should keep in mind the following:

- The "shelf-life" of a description or analysis of the state of lifelong learning in any one country is short; there is ongoing debate as to its operational objectives, and institutional arrangements.
- The descriptions and analyses focus more on financing issues related to formal education and training systems and institutions, than on those related to non-formal learning because the former relate most directly to the existing legal roles and responsibilities, require that legal and regulatory change precede institutional change and, of course, are more easily observed.
- Because the country reports follow a common scope agreed to by national experts, in order to facilitate comparison, the synthesis report may not provide a view that reflects fully the relative emphasis given to certain issues within a particular country.

© OECD 2000

Chapter 1

Goals, Objectives, and Priorities

The goal of achieving lifelong learning is ambitious in its aims to engage all citizens in the process of learning. It is complex because it breaks with past education reforms by defining in new ways the content, place, timing and duration of learning. Perhaps more fundamentally, it shifts the focus of policy from institutions to learners. In this context, the answer to the question of how societies will find the resources for lifelong learning will depend on how society defines the new mandate, and the priority it is given.

This chapter examines the progress selected OECD Member countries have made in specifying their objectives and strategies, and estimating the resources they require.

From advocacy to action

The importance of the issue of the affordability of lifelong learning for all depends first on how ambitious or modest the vision is and the extent to which it is implemented. If lifelong learning for all means simply to ensure that everyone has access to books, the costs are far more manageable than a goal that envisions that all adults have the reading skills needed for employment and self-directed learning.

OECD Education Ministers were, in fact, fairly ambitious in the goals that they agreed to assign to lifelong learning for all, and in outlining strategies for achieving those goals. But, in order to grasp the resource implications of the mandate, it is necessary to identify the operational objectives that need to be met, and to evaluate their costs. This report aims to go beyond advocacy, and to examine practical issues that are confronting OECD policy makers, who have accepted the need for lifelong learning and are now facing the overriding practical question of the political arena, how to pay for it.

The discussion below examines first the policy making process by which individual countries evaluate where they are starting and establish targets, it summarises the progress to date towards defining lifelong learning targets, and then it considers

© OECD 2000

the likely costs of reaching those targets. Chapters 2 and 3 then consider how those targets might be made more affordable, in order to make them more achievable.

Stages of formulating and implementing policy for lifelong learning

The idea of lifelong learning for all is now very high on the policy agenda of most OECD countries. As a mobilising concept, "lifelong learning for all" is self-explanatory. It can be interpreted, and advocated, in psychological, social, cultural and economic terms. However, in order for substantial progress to occur, the broad goals have to be translated into operational objectives that lend themselves to being implemented with respect not only to policy, institutional, programmatic, and behavioural considerations, but with respect to resource requirements. In considering what total resources to devote to lifelong learning, how to find them, how to allocate them, and how to ensure that they are used effectively and efficiently, the meanings given to the term, and the values underlying them, need to be clear. As with education generally, but more acutely because lifelong learning aims to shift the centre of gravity of educational effort towards adults and older people who have their own interests and preferences already formed, the competing claims of education for self development, education for an improved civil society and education for wealth creation cannot be ignored. In addition, at the operational level where ideas become policies and policies become practice, policy technicians cannot avoid asking practical questions such as:

- In what ways does it impinge on compulsory schooling or other initial education of young people in the formal school system?
- How much informal and casual learning can be included?
- What should be the balance of economic, social and cultural considerations in any particular policy initiative?
- Which public and private agencies are involved in the policy formulation and implementation processes (including mobilising the resources)?

One indicator of the seriousness and maturity of its lifelong learning debate in the broader political arena is the extent to which a country is examining specific issues that go beyond advocacy. It is possible to set out five broad stages in the development of lifelong learning policy:

- Advocacy, that is mobilising support for the concept.
- Analysis, that is deconstructing the general term to consider the various constituents of a lifelong learning policy and the various actors involved in its formulation and implementation.
- Prioritising, that is deciding the priority to be given to each of the numerous claims which can be made under the general heading, lifelong learning.

- Allocating resources, this includes both raising resources and distributing them according to the priorities that have been established.
- Evaluating the effectiveness and efficiency of resource use in relation to the priorities that have been established.

These are not, of course, completely discrete stages: it is possible to be at stage five in one set of activities and at stage one in another. However, the overriding impression from the country reports is that OECD countries are mostly somewhere between the first and second stage with a few moving towards stages three and four. There are few examples of stage five types of activity.

Overview of the country goals for lifelong learning

In 1996 the OECD suggested five basic rationales for lifelong learning:
- The learning economy argument, which recognises the extent to which OECD economies and societies have moved towards a dependence on the creation and manipulation of knowledge, information and ideas.
- The ubiquity and speed of technological change and of growth in knowledge and information.
- Growing recognition that traditional redistribution policies are inadequate because they have ignored the life-cycle patterns of income of individuals.
- An "active policies" argument based on the idea that an underlying broad aim should be to move away from essentially passive policies based on transfer payments – especially in response to unemployment – towards active policies that contribute directly to the formation of human capital and to the psychological and social well-being of individuals.
- The "social cohesion" argument which claims that, because of the importance of learning in knowledge intensive societies, those who miss out, either initially or later on, suffer effective social exclusion (OECD, 1996).

All the countries that took part in this study recognise the potential of lifelong learning as a response to these five policy concerns, but there are differences of emphasis and priorities between them. Table 1.1 summarises the main aims identified by national authorities. Most countries stress the need for a learning economy and the speed of technological change. However, in the countries where existing institutional arrangements already provide substantial opportunities for lifelong learning (Denmark, Finland, Japan, the Netherlands, Sweden), there is strong interest in the life-cycle distribution of educational needs and opportunities. In some cases, current initiatives focus only on segments where opportunities are limited. These conceptions of lifelong learning have an influence on whether lifelong learning is seen as something new, requiring net additional resources, or as something that can be supported through the reallocation of existing educational and training resources.

© OECD 2000

Table 1.1. **How do countries articulate their lifelong learning goals?**

Austria: Priority to strengthening vocational education and training.	"Lifelong learning" has been featured since the early 1990s in the working agreements of the governing coalition and social partners. It refers principally to vocational and further education and training; social and cultural aspects are secondary. Objectives are quite specific. They include increased opportunities for the workforce, in particular by establishing *Fachhochschul* courses; equal status of adult education and training in the education system; expanded and improved forms of co-operation between public and private institutions; increased access for disadvantaged persons; permeability between the dual system and the other education and training tracks; re-employment rights to permit employed persons to participate in continuing education and training; improvements of the apprenticeship training by means of the introduction of "group trades", the intensified use of interplant training workshops, the promotion of foreign language instruction, and the support of creativity and co-operation in dual training.
Czech Republic: Immediate concern with strengthening initial education.	Lifelong learning is seen as a comprehensive process of vital importance: "The government considers its integral goal to be its contribution to the Czech society becoming a society of learning. The idea of a learning society draws on the presumption that the qualifications of people are currently becoming a basic production factor (Country Report – Czech Republic)". It covers learners of all ages, though the process can be divided into two fundamental phases, namely initial education of all young people in the framework of the formal education system, and all subsequent continuing education and learning. Its purpose includes both the education preparing the student for his/her future profession and aimed at the application of innovations, economic growth, etc., and the education aimed at the personal cultivation of individuals or the cultivation of community life. Continuing (further) education includes both the education of the employed and of the unemployed, and retired persons. It takes place in formal settings, provided by the state and private institutions, as well as in churches and enterprises. It is financed by varied sources. In the short and medium term, the policy pre-occupations of public officials and social partners have been with the formal sector for initial education.
Denmark: Improve opportunities for adults.	Lifelong learning is viewed as a mandate for ensuring adequate learning opportunities for adults. There is a long and strong tradition of adult learning. A measure adopted in 1995 mentions the importance of initial education providing a sound foundation for further learning; and stresses wider opportunities to be provided through rationalisation of services by formal education institutions in order to allow freer choice by adults among learning opportunities as well as co-operation with industry. It calls for expanded provision of learning opportunities, greater use of appropriate technologies, greater transparency of learning, better information on learning opportunities, financial support for learners, and special support for learners with limited educational background. There is strong support for early childhood education and development, and sound preparation for young persons; however, policies in those areas are neither driven by, nor evaluated in terms of lifelong learning objectives.
Finland: Broad social and economic goals; initiatives cut across the age spectrum.	Lifelong learning ensures broadly based and continuous learning throughout society. The concept concerns the learning careers of individuals, the activities of communities and policies to promote learning. The government's development plan for the period 1995-2000 emphasises the multiple purposes of learning, and need for it to be widely accessible. Aims to: offer one year of pre-school education for all children before the comprehensive school; maintain high upper-secondary completion rates and increase proportion of those continuing in post-compulsory study; revise secondary vocational diplomas, with more emphasis on on-the-job learning and apprenticeships; complete reform of polytechnic sector, and expand

Table 1.1. **How do countries articulate their lifelong learning goals?** (*cont.*)

	places, so that 60-65% of secondary completers can enter tertiary education; increase adult education leading to qualifications; increase training places by about 50%; expand other forms of continuing education.
Hungary: Strengthen formal education.	Lifelong learning is embodied in the "Strategy for the long-term development of Hungarian public education". It concerns modernisation of public education, and improvements in content that equip students to upgrade their skills and knowledge. The term includes organised learning for adults, subsequent to the completion of formal education, mainly related to the workplace. Non-formal self-education is not included. In the immediate term, the government is focusing on vocational training for young persons; training for the unemployed, at-risk workers, and education opportunities for socially disadvantaged persons and ethnic minorities are expanding.
Italy: Better initial education; more flexibility for adults.	Lifelong learning was introduced as a policy objective by the government in 1996, in consultation with the social partners. The concept addresses concerns about the quality and relevance of initial education, the gulf between formal education and the economy, relatively low level of education levels of adults and young persons, and the need for ensuring that the learning process is more individualised and flexible.
Japan: Learner is central; policy responsibilities are complex.	"Lifelong integrated learning" was introduced in the 1960s, in co-operation with the Ministry of Education, as a means for reforming Japan's school-centred education system, and improving re-training opportunities for adult workers, thus compensating for declining numbers of young persons entering the labour force. It also was seen as a tool for regional development. The concept of "lifelong learning" emerged in the early 1980s; the concept was further developed by an education reform council reporting to the prime minister, placing the learner at the centre, and charging the formal education system with preparing individuals to learn throughout their lives. Policies now implicate the Ministries of Labour, Health and Welfare, Construction, and Industry and Trade, as well as education authorities.
Korea: Lifelong learning is central to economic development.	While the concept of lifelong learning has long been valued philosophically in Korea, in practice it has been viewed as a luxury. The economic crisis of the mid-late 1990s (including restructuring of industry and high rates of unemployment) has pushed the government to pursue a more instrumental approach to it. The recently enacted Lifelong Learning Act expands job-related education and training activities for employed worker and the unemployed. At the same time, education reforms are being pursued to diversify student choice in schools, and increase learning opportunities that are accessible at any time, any place, and through varied media.
Netherlands: Improve opportunities for adults.	Elements of lifelong learning have been long established in the Netherlands. By the 1980s there were part-time alternatives for regular secondary and tertiary education, a diversified field of liberal adult education often run by the voluntary sector, a well organised private sector especially in the field of correspondence education and the relatively uncharted sector of on-the-job training. There was virtually no policy for the post-initial phase. By the early 1990s adult basic education for people with little previous or no schooling, and the Open University had been added. There also was rapid growth in training for the unemployed during the late 1980s and early 1990s. In the 1990s there have been efforts to more closely link vocational training and business, to better translate labour market needs into school goals and curricula, to facilitate entry of non-public providers to learning markets, and to increase transparency of qualification requirements and learning outside the formal

© OECD 2000

Table 1.1. **How do countries articulate their lifelong learning goals?** (*cont.*)

	education sector. The lifelong learning programme presented in 1998 focuses on employability of employees and job seekers; employability of teaching staff; and prevention of disadvantages and reorientation of the education system towards lifelong learning.
Norway: Competence development in different settings.	Though there is no single, comprehensive definition of "lifelong learning" in Norway, the concept has expanded to embrace the complete life span including basic education for children and young people. The current political and social debates on lifelong learning is premised on the assumption that knowledge and skills must be continually updated in order to improve employability; and increasing the accumulated competence of society as a whole to improve macro-economic performance. Actions being considered focus on improving competence and training in various contexts and across policy areas including: expansion and reforms in the initial education and training system, whether at primary, secondary or higher level; active labour market policy; the workplace. There is a growing awareness that learning occurs in different contexts and life situations. The conditions under which training occurs and the systems for documentation and assessment of non-formal learning are important questions in the Norwegian debate on education and training.
Sweden: Serves multiple objectives, requires better linkages between different policies.	Lifelong learning is an attitude to learning. It goes further than the concept of recurrent education insofar as it covers the formal educational system, from pedagogical measures in the early years of the pre-school up to studies at university and popular adult education for young people and adults, as well as learning opportunities at work. The great challenge is to create amongst all citizens a desire to learn and the opportunities for realising this. The foundation for this attitude to lifelong learning must be built during the child's early years in pre-school and later permeate the formal educational system, as well as attitudes to competence development in working life and opportunities for participating in study circles during leisure time. Lifelong learning is being pursued to help individuals and societies adapt to a changing economic context, to link learning and working life, and to prepare individuals to participate in a society that is increasingly knowledge intensive and multicultural.

Source: Country reports.

Many of the countries are also concerned about unemployment and convinced of the need to use lifelong learning to address this problem. This is linked both to issues of active employment policies and social cohesion, lest the unemployed become an "excluded" group. There is also a broad consensus on the need to retrain workers who have had little previous education and those who are in danger of losing their jobs if they are not re-skilled. This appears to be the fundamental requirement in all the countries for training in the workplace.

Country-specific considerations

Although there are clearly discernible convergent trends in relation to lifelong learning in all the country reports, there are also concerns arising from country-specific contexts. Lifelong learning is seen as a policy response to specific problems in different countries. For example, in the Czech Republic and in Hungary it is a way of coping with changes resulting from the emergence from Communist regimes and aligning themselves with what are seen as the socially advanced European countries. Austria is concerned about lifelong learning as a very important aspect of economic, democratic and cultural development. In Sweden lifelong learning is important for allowing individuals to be active participants in both working life and the democratic process. Norway stresses the need to take a more strategic approach to adult education because of the importance of improving competence for economic activity and employment. In Japan, there is a particular concern about the effects of demographic changes and its ageing population. The Japanese report also takes the broadest view of what constitutes lifelong learning and conceptualises it in part as a lifestyle commodity encompassing attendance at conferences and a wide variety of recreational activities. One corollary of this is that the Japanese report is the most likely to consider a wide variety of private expenditures as forming part of the resources available for lifelong learning.

The authors of the country reports agree on the growing policy salience of lifelong learning since 1990. However, there appears to be a much longer tradition of public policy debate around the issue and strategic planning in some countries (*e.g.* Denmark, Finland, Italy, Japan, the Netherlands and Sweden) than in others. In some countries, there is no means, as yet, of taking a holistic view of lifelong learning (*e.g.* Austria, Hungary), because all the phases of the education system are still largely seen as separate entities.

Varied views of the functions of lifelong learning

There are very different conceptions of the function of lifelong learning in country reports – from being a project for creating a more equitable and democratic society (*e.g.* Sweden), to tackling political and social as well as economic problems (*e.g.* Denmark), to providing the capability to change the whole system of education (*e.g.* Italy and Japan), to addressing deficits in education in a very discrete part of the system (*e.g.* Hungary and Norway). In most there is seen to be a need to change individuals' views of the role and importance of lifelong learning, as well as making structural changes to education and training systems. These would be categorised as part of the advocacy stage of the policy process that is explained in the preceding section. However, not all countries appear to take such a broad approach. There is a range of different conceptions of lifelong learning. In Japan, there is a very comprehensive idea of lifelong learning that includes non-vocational liberal adult education. In Finland and Sweden, formal lifelong learning opportunities are seen as part of a strategy for tackling societal and political problems as well as economic issues and significant national debates and policies are already in evidence. Denmark defines it more narrowly in terms of adult learning, "(…) as the principle that all citizens should have the opportunity to return to education throughout life". In Austria and Norway, there is a focus on work-based education and training and qualification levels. In Hungary, "non-formal self education" is clearly not currently considered to be part of lifelong learning. These approaches we would consider typical of stages two and three of the policy process. They are beginning the process of analysis and prioritisation.

Some country reports consider the whole education system from pre-school onwards to constitute lifelong learning (e.g. Finland and Sweden) because philosophically they do not wish to narrow the concept of lifelong learning. Others start at "foundation learning" but focus largely on upper secondary, tertiary and adult education. In some reports there is little on the public education of adults (e.g. the Czech Republic) – this has been seen as something for employers or individuals. There is some correlation between those countries which have a strong tradition of adult education and those which now have a more holistic view of lifelong learning.

The perceived need for partnerships for lifelong learning

There is fairly general recognition of the fact that government, by itself, cannot create a system of lifelong learning and that public funding alone cannot finance the undertaking. There is, therefore, seen to be a need to involve employers and, in some cases, trade unions, more actively and effectively in strategies for lifelong learning, and to seek substantial private funding. A social partnership model is more highly developed and formalised in some countries (e.g. Austria, Denmark, the Netherlands and Norway) than in others, such as Japan, where there is more trust in private provision. Similarly policies and strategies for increasing the proportion of private funding for lifelong learning are more evident in some countries than others, although all recognise the need to do more in this area. These may be seen as moving beyond stage three to grappling with the issues of resource allocation decisions that comprise stage four.

There are obviously different definitions of lifelong learning and different discourses to communicate broader and narrower conceptions of it – but there is a core of common agreement about its functions, importance and the need for future development. However, the details vary considerably. The extent to which national government is seen as having an overriding responsibility to steer policy varies greatly, as do the perceived roles of regional and local government. These are clearly related to the constitutional situation in different countries. In addition, each country has its own economic and social priorities for lifelong learning to address and this naturally shapes both its current policy approach and its priorities for future development.

However, even in those countries which are wrestling with stages three and four of the policy process and have begun to develop an operational national strategy for lifelong learning (e.g. Finland, Italy, Japan, the Netherlands and Sweden), strategic planning of this kind has only been in place for one or two years. Many of the policies and initiatives which this report describes, therefore, are still at an early stage of development. In the majority of cases, efficiency savings, enhancement of quality and the mobilisation of additional resources for lifelong learning, must be seen, at this point in time, in terms of anticipated rather than actual outcomes. Moreover, in some of the reports (*e.g.* Finland and the Netherlands), there was some uncertainty about future policy directions because of imminent general elections which highlights another uncertainty of any policy analysis in OECD countries.

From policy goals to operational objectives

In *Lifelong Learning for All* (OECD, 1996), the OECD set the following strategic goals for lifelong education policies:

- Enlarging access to high-quality early childhood education.
- Revitalising foundation learning in primary and secondary schools.
- Overcoming problems of transition from education to work.
- Encouraging adult learning.
- Addressing the lack of coherence in the system.
- Renewing the resources and "assets" of the system (particularly staff).

The key roles of governments in this process would be to:

- Redefine the roles and responsibilities of Education Ministries and their partners.
- Encourage the appropriate human resources, institutional arrangements, and knowledge base to provide high-quality lifelong learning, in formal as well as non-formal settings.
- Ensure adequate financing arrangements to implement an inclusive programme of lifelong learning and providing sufficient opportunities and incentives to the partners in the system.

About half the countries considered in this report currently claim to have made significant progress in establishing a national strategy for lifelong learning with operational objectives. Denmark, Finland, Italy, Japan, Korea, the Netherlands, Norway and Sweden all report measurable progress in terms of allocation of resources in the light of lifelong learning priorities, though many of the reports are not clear about the amount of resources involved, and the degree of comprehensiveness of the strategies varies considerably. In Denmark between the mid-1980s and mid-1990s, spending on adults grew more than twice as fast as spending in initial education (including higher education); growth in adult enrolments also outpaced all other sectors. In Norway a government white paper on "The Competence Reform" has put forward a long-term strategy for adult learning and a lifelong learning perspective. Furthermore, comprehensive reforms, based on a lifelong learning perspective, are being implemented in primary and lower

© OECD 2000

secondary education, upper secondary education and partly also in higher education. The apprenticeship system has been re-established to strengthen links between education and work.

Assigning responsibilities and co-ordinating roles

The authors in several countries express a concern to co-ordinate disparate policies related to lifelong learning, especially in those countries where there is no national strategy as yet (*e.g.* Austria through its Board of Compulsory Education and Training; the Czech Republic through formulation of government policy for lifelong learning). Where strategic goals and objectives have been explicitly laid out in country reports, they tend to reflect some or all of those outlined by the OECD with a particular emphasis on problems of transition from education to work, encouraging adult learning and addressing the lack of coherence in the system. All the country reports claim that all three key instruments identified by OECD are being used to a greater or lesser degree for implementing national strategies.

There are widely different views about the role of government in stimulating and supporting lifelong learning. At one extreme, existing arrangements are seen in Denmark, by and large, as being satisfactory. The Danish authorities seem broadly satisfied with the breadth and volume of existing arrangements. There seems to be little importance to the question of how to mobilise additional, non-public financial resources for lifelong learning activities. The view in the Ministry of Education and Labour has been that the total volume of education and training currently provided is about right, and that the current division of financing responsibilities is appropriate (perhaps not too surprising in view of the relatively high personal tax rates). However, there has been increased concern lately over signs that growth in demand for training in some areas may outpace the capacity of the ministries to pay for it. If this happens it will increase pressure to ration opportunities, reallocate resources from other areas, and or limit the public share of total costs. However, all reports have amongst their objectives the need to focus on co-operation between the public and private sectors and also to decentralise decision-making to the education provider level. One of the most widely mentioned objectives is ensuring that national government plays a role in encouraging equity in provision. Many of the reports recognise that current systems have not succeeded in creating equal opportunities for access to education and training and that, without regulation, market approaches may exacerbate this situation. It is generally assumed that government will always have a safety net function, regardless of how much private investment is made in lifelong learning. The Netherlands report, for example, looks at the specific lifelong learning needs of older workers, long-term unemployed and women returning to the labour force and concludes that there is a particular role for incentives for these groups.

© OECD 2000

There is a general preference to concentrate on strengthening the demand for lifelong learning, rather than assuming any particular role in improving institutional arrangements for providing learning opportunities. Many of the reports underline the importance of national governments favouring policies to encourage individuals to participate in lifelong learning. Different countries' approaches to incentives are looked at in more detail in Chapter 3, but objectives in this area include, for example, consideration of tax incentives in Italy, Japan and Hungary; and of educational credits in Italy, Japan and Korea.

One widespread concern is the lack of co-ordination of the various contributors to lifelong learning. In the Austrian report, for example, there is a call for better harmonisation of the various parts of the post-secondary sector. The Czech report also calls for an assessment of the possibilities arising from other partnerships and their legislative regulation. Japan is keen to encourage inter-ministerial co-operation. Hungary too is aware of this problem and is taking steps to ensure that the Departments of Education and Labour work in a more co-ordinated manner.

Lifelong learning as a governmental level conception has not been formulated yet across OECD countries, but programmes and actions have been realised in the second half of the 1990s that can be seen as important elements in a comprehensive conception.

All the country reports recognise the need to involve employers more actively in lifelong learning, but proposals for achieving this vary widely. They include:

- improvement in co-operation between education and the world of work (*e.g.* Austria, Denmark, Italy, Hungary, Norway, the Netherlands and Sweden);
- incentives and support for employers to provide training (*e.g.* Italy and the Netherlands through the Investors in People initiative and tax measures); and
- continued support for the levy system in the Netherlands.

In Sweden, one goal of recent and ongoing reforms is to "bring about co-operation between policies for education, the labour market and industry in order to develop a coherent infrastructure in the area of education and lifelong learning". In Italy, a National Labour Agreement in 1996 brought "the lifelong learning concept officially and legitimately in the policies of both government and social bodies". It is recognised that in order to implement this it is necessary to ensure co-ordination between national, regional and local government.

The need for collaboration between central, regional and local governments is frequently emphasised in several reports. However, it is also possible to detect a note of agnosticism here and there. For example, as stated in the Dutch report:

"Finally efforts have been made to strengthen the public infrastructure of vocational and adult education by the development of strong and relatively inde-

© OECD 2000

pendent regional educational centres. This has led to the formation of large centres, with a strong regional presence and a promise to cater for the needs of different target groups, young as well as adult. Whether they will fulfil that promise is a matter for the future."

Other specific objectives

In addition to these organisational issues, there are common areas where many countries wish to increase participation in particular aspects of lifelong learning: frequent mentions are made of higher education, education in the workplace and provision for those with lowest levels of qualification and unemployed. Several countries want to increase rates of higher education participation and achievement (*e.g.* Austria, Italy, Japan and Sweden): in some cases, there is a particular focus on a specific type of HE, for example, Austria and Italy focus on technical, scientific and professional tertiary education.

In many countries there is also a clear recognition of the importance of foundation learning as a basis for lifelong learning. In the Netherlands, for example:

"People with low levels of initial education are clearly under-represented in the various types of post-initial education and training. Both in training of the employed and the unemployed, the relative participation of the lower educated is about half of the average. Even in higher distance education, which was originally meant as a second chance type education, about half of the participants have already reached (another direction of) higher education. This means that post-initial education tends to increase existing differences in levels of education instead of reducing these."

Also, in the Netherlands, there has been a debate about the notion of entitlement to a minimum or starter qualification (which may be described as a minimum level of achievement for everyone before the end of their initial education). It is recognised, however, that if this entitlement were extended to all adults, the cost implications would be enormous.

In Finland, Italy and the Netherlands there is a desire to increase initial post-compulsory education participation rates – in the former case with an emphasis on increasing the importance of work-based or work-related options and, in the two latter cases, with a focus on reducing drop-out rates. It must be remembered, however, that for many people there is a conception of lifelong learning as being primarily about post-initial education and training, and this perception may have influenced some of the authors.

Austria lays particular stress on institutional changes (*e.g.* expansion and co-operation of public and private institutions; equal status for adult education/training in the education system), and improving access of individuals in the workplace to learning opportunities. Finland prioritises one year of pre-school education for all. Hungary wants to increase compulsory education to 18.

Lifelong learning gaps and participation targets for closing them: evaluating different scenarios

In an attempt to highlight the kinds of resource questions that arise in relation to lifelong learning, the OECD Secretariat prepared for the Education Ministerial meeting in 1996 crude estimates of the costs of implementing certain aspects of lifelong learning. The estimates were calculated on the basis of participation targets (which took account of the proportion of different sub-groups that was at risk in the labour market, and demographic trends affecting the size of such groups), and the costs of achieving the targets (based on unit costs of relevant education and training activities). Those estimates assumed that lifelong learning policies would involve achieving certain participation rates with regard to formal initial education for young persons, and with regard to participation by poorly qualified adults in training. The analysis was intended to illustrate how the resources required for lifelong learning varies with different configurations of goals and objectives, and strategies for achieving them. Box 1.1 describes the approach in more detail.

The Member countries that prepared reports on alternative approaches to financing lifelong learning agreed to undertake a similar analysis to that undertaken in 1996 by the OECD Secretariat. It was agreed that even if countries had not yet specified objectives with regard to implementation of lifelong learning, it would be useful to investigate how resource requirements might vary under different assumptions about the content of lifelong learning policies, and whom they might affect. The majority of the country reports refer to the participation targets based on assumptions posed by the Secretariat in 1996, in order to estimate "participation gaps" that need to be addressed if lifelong learning for all is to be come a reality. Some – Austria and the Netherlands, for example – adjust the objectives. Norway and, to a lesser extent Sweden, provide estimates that are based on policy targets.

With some adaptations of the targets suggested by the OECD to conform to the structures of national education systems, there were relatively few problems with the first four "initial education" components: the countries concerned have considerable experience of submitting information on these categories to the OECD. However, at tertiary level, many countries used enrolment rates as a proxy for completion rates so it is possible that the real extent of participation gaps may have been underestimated. There are big differences between those countries where the targets have been or very nearly have been met, such as Japan, and those where there remains a considerable distance to go (see Annex 2).

© OECD 2000

Box 1.1. **Evaluating the implications of different strategies for implementing lifelong learning**

In 1996, in order to provide a basis for an initial debate by Education Ministers about the financing and affordability of lifelong learning, the OECD Secretariat prepared a series of hypothetical policy scenarios for achieving the goal of lifelong learning for all. The scenarios were estimates of the size of the participation and expenditure gaps that had to be closed in order "to make lifelong learning for all a reality". The scenarios were calculated according to different definitions of lifelong learning that varied with respect to which groups of individuals were served, and what percentage of persons within those groups were served. The scenarios also differed with respect to what level unit costs were assumed to be (for definitions used in evaluating need for lifelong learning, and policy targets for evaluating participation gaps, see Annex 1): the scenarios were not intended to provide precise estimates of the operational objectives implied by lifelong learning. Rather, their purpose was to focus the debate on three distinct questions:

– How ambitious a definition of lifelong learning for all could societies afford?

– Could they afford the unit costs that are observed in historical data?

– Would they finance it with existing resources, or would additional sources of finance be needed?

The Secretariat analysis suggested that under a variety of scenarios, "lifelong learning for all" was likely to be an expensive goal to achieve (OECD, 1996, pp. 259-265). Without implying which policy choices were appropriate, the analysis suggested that virtually any scenario posed important resource challenges in many countries. To meet such challenges, there is a need for major improvements in the cost-effectiveness of provision and returns to various forms of lifelong learning, and improved mechanisms to make it easier for various actors, individuals and employers especially, to finance it.

When national experts on financing lifelong learning first discussed the guidelines for preparing country reports, they agreed that it would be useful to prepare their own estimates of the "price tag" for lifelong learning. It was hoped that such re-estimates could take fuller account of particular priorities and more detailed data than were available to the OECD Secretariat. In the event, that has proven difficult. First, it often has been difficult, for political reasons, to specify the lifelong learning mandate in terms of the population to be served and the service to be provided. Second, it has been difficult to develop credible estimates of unit costs. This has been because there is little basis for estimating *marginal costs* of future changes in formal education systems (historical cost data based on outlays per pupil, for example, are not particularly helpful). Also, there are little data available on costs in the non-formal settings in which lifelong learning occurs.

As a result, some countries have not estimated any gaps or the costs of filling them. Others have tried to re-calculate them on the basis of hypothetical scenarios prepared by the OECD. Others have prepared entirely new scenarios based on their own interpretation of national priorities and experience.

Goals, Objectives, and Priorities

> Box 1.1. **Evaluating the implications of different strategies for implementing lifelong learning** (*cont.*)
>
> The picture that emerges is fairly consistent with the original OECD Secretariat analysis: lifelong learning is likely to be an expensive goal to achieve no matter how it is defined. Progress will depend on raising rates of return (increasing benefits, reducing costs) to learning for individuals, enterprises and societies in order to strengthen incentives to invest in lifelong learning; and finding ways of easing the liquidity constraints that individuals and employers face when trying to finance lifelong learning.

Foundation and tertiary education

In Japan, with over 97% of students advancing to high school, we can say there are no gaps at this level. Similarly, with tertiary education, even if the target were set at 60%, we can say that effectively there are no gaps since, at present, including special training schools with a post-secondary level curriculum, the tertiary advancement rate is almost 69%. Within adult education, we can also say that there are no gaps pertaining to basic literacy, as literacy is nearly universal in Japan. In Denmark, the lifelong learning mandate is seen as being fulfilled through ongoing reforms in initial education and continued expansion of adult opportunities.

Another country where very little additional effort is required to meet the initial education targets is Sweden where, in 1997, "around 87% of all 20 year-olds had completed upper secondary education". The Swedish report also shows that in all age groups up to the mid-40s, over 80% of the population have reached ISCED level 3 or higher. However, the Swedish report makes the important point that, while expansion of numbers is not an issue, there is a need to take measures to stimulate more pupils in upper secondary school to complete their education more quickly. The targets for tertiary education are also near to being met. In 1997, 28% of the 25-year-old population had completed at least a short university degree and current enrolments and immediate plans are expected to raise this to 35%. During the same period, the number with "long university degrees is expected to rise from 13% to 18.5%".

The Netherlands report elaborates the OECD targets in considerable detail to adapt them to the Dutch situation. After making these adjustments and making separate calculations for each of the three main branches of education and training up to ISCED 3, it is estimated that enrolments would, in 1996, need to have been about 7% higher to have met the targets in full. For tertiary education in total, the increase required would have been about 10% (Box 1.2 and Table 1.2).

© OECD 2000

Box 1.2. **Estimating participation gaps:
the example of the Netherlands**

Taking as an example the Dutch situation, the OECD targets were adapted to close the existing gap in training of lower educated employees and to provide more initial education to reduce participation gaps in the future. In the Netherlands it is not possible to complete all types of upper secondary education by the age of 18. Therefore, the age at which this 90% target has to be achieved is set at 27. This corresponds to the national policy aim of getting (almost) everyone to the so called "starting qualification". Of all persons aged 27 in 1996, 26.35% or 67 660 did not have a "starting qualification". Correcting for the 10% assumed not to be able to reach that level, the total participation gap is 41 960 persons. This number has to be divided over their present level of basic education, junior general secondary education and junior vocational training. It is assumed that 60% of those with only basic education belong to the "less able". It is important to note that this participation gap applies to each year cohort. It should be noted that the future completion gap is overstated, because the cohort size of younger generations is much smaller than the number of current 30 year-olds.

For tertiary education, rather than accept the disaggregated OECD figures, it is more realistic to assume an overall target of 30% for all sectors of tertiary education combined. In total, 19 550 additional students are needed each year to reach the target of 30%.

According to the OECD, 20% of adults with educational attainment of ISCED level 2 or below should participate in basic adult education each year. Younger generations tend to be better educated and therefore the group in need of basic adult education is smaller. Furthermore, the participation rate of younger generations is already higher than for older people, so a relatively small group has to participate in order to reach the target. A more ambitious target rate of 30% might be set for poorly educated adults under 45 and economically it would seem more effective to start with training the younger generations (under age 45) who are currently out of the labour force. Of adults not in the labour force with an educational attainment less than ISCED level 3, only 6.7% participate in adult education during one year, far below the target of 20%. Of those over 45, fewer than 5% undertake a course in any year. Of those between 25 and 44 who are out of the labour force, almost 12% participate in adult education in any one year. This, combined with the higher educational attainment of younger generations, will help close the gap in the future. Amongst the long-term unemployed, annual participation was 27%. Compared to the OECD target of 100% (161 500 persons), this represents a substantial participation gap. The authors of the Dutch report therefore chose an alternative target rate of 50% that results in a participation gap of 51 000 persons. Avoiding double counting of the training measures already proposed for those with low educational attainment indicated above, this gives a net enrolment gap of 37 700.

© OECD 2000

Table 1.2. **Participation gaps in the Netherlands**

Educational levels below upper secondary	Percent of population aged 27[1]	Population aged 27 at these levels	(Reduction to)	Gap
Basic education	7.46	19 160	11 500	7 660
First level general secondary education (MAVO)	6.22	15 970	2 800	13 170
Junior vocational education (VBO)	12.67	32 530	11 400	21 130
Total	26.35[2]	67 660	25 700[3]	41 960

1. Total population aged 27 is 256 883 in 1996.
2. This is an overestimation of the number below upper secondary education, because these figures include part of those who have attained an apprenticeship diploma. However, more exact figures excluding all those with apprenticeship training do not exist.
3. 0% of total population aged 27.

Source: Country report on the Netherlands.

In contrast to the Dutch situation, Hungary and the Czech Republic face impossible challenges. In Hungary, it is estimated that to meet the OECD targets in pre-primary, primary and secondary education, enrolments would need to rise by about 14%, and, in higher education, the increase would need to be 90%. The Czech Republic estimates that 67% of 15-18 year-olds are enrolled in 1998 and, if enrolments stay constant till 2005, this will have risen to 75% as a result of declines in the size of the age group. In tertiary education, total enrolment would rise from 11.7% today to 14.5% by 2005. This would need to more than double to meet the OECD targets.

Austria is between these extremes: the ISCED 3 targets were effectively met by the mid-1990s, but the tertiary education enrolment targets are far from being met. In 1995/96, enrolment rates for 18-21 year-olds, were only 2.5% in non-university tertiary education, and 13.8% in university education. Figures for 22-25 year-olds were 2.1% and 15.5% respectively. However, these figures underestimate tertiary enrolments to the extent that they exclude enrolments in BHS – secondary technical and vocational colleges – that the EU classifies as "post-secondary technical vocational education". Thus persons who complete BHS but go no further are now counted in any tertiary enrolments; if they were, tertiary enrolments would be somewhat higher, though still short of the target. However, a new policy in the early 1990s established a system of *Fachhochschulen* (which offer shorter, more vocational courses than universities). Full-time first year enrolments there more than doubled between 1995/96 and 1997/98, and are expected to grow sharply in the future.

Adult education

The identification of participation gaps for poorly qualified adults, for long-term unemployed adults and for job-related training courses proved more difficult for most countries to calculate, and a much wider variety of approaches is used in the country reports. All the reports suggest deficiencies in relation to perceived needs, but there is little uniformity in arriving at the estimates.

The most comprehensive treatment is in the Netherlands report, which presents detailed estimates of the targets for increases in participation of poorly qualified adults in adult education, and labour market training (Table 1.3).

Hungary estimates participation gaps based on serving 100% of those persons with less than basic literacy levels, 100% of unskilled unemployed adults, and 40% of other employed adults. In the Czech report, adult basic education is not considered to be a problem because, for some decades, basic education and basic literacy have been available for all. There is some concern about functional literacy to meet the needs of the workplace and it is suggested that annual enrolment levels similar to tertiary education are needed to deal with this. About 15% of the unemployed receive training each year. This figure would need to double to meet the targets set in the report. However, since no figures are available for the long term unemployed, it is difficult to compare this with the OECD targets. Similarly a doubling of other job-related training for adults is recommended.

Table 1.3. **Participation targets in the Netherlands**
(Attainment gaps by all relevant sectors within adult education)

	Population (thousands)	Percentage served	Target (%)	Participation gap (number)
Adult education for poorly qualified (below ISCED 3)				
Not in the labour force (25-44)	513	11.5	30	94 900
Not in the labour force (45-64)	1 051	4.3	10	59 900
Education for long-term unemployed[1]				
All long-term unemployed	221	27	50	51 000
Of which lower educated	102	13	50	38 000
Others	119	39	50	13 000
Job-related training				
Job-related training (25-64), below ISCED 3	1 481	20.8	30	136 300
Other employees (at or above ISCED 3) following job-related training (25-64)	3 922	39.0	40	39 200

1. On the basis of the Statistics Netherlands definition of unemployed. If the definition "registered unemployed" have been used, the number of long-term unemployed would have been lower and participation higher. Therefore the gaps would be lower, too.

Source: Country report on the Netherlands.

Japan faces a different situation. Employment-related training is undertaken by employers and it is assumed that they do as much training as is economically justified. According to a survey reported by the Ministry of Education, Science and Culture, 48% of adults undertake non employment-related education or training during the course of a year, but 65% would like to. This is taken as the basis of a calculation showing a participation gap in adult education that would require an expansion of provision of about 17%.

In Austria, there are no detailed data on preferences and actual participation in continuing education and training more recent than 1989, making it difficult to calculate a participation gap on the basis of unmet need. In the absence of such data, the participation gap is estimated as the difference between the overall annual participation of 25.8%, according to survey results from 1996, and the 40% target used by the OECD Secretariat as the basis for its gap analysis. This works out to approximately 543 600 persons. A large share of that participation gap would appear to be among poorly qualified workers. Although there are no data on annual participation rates by occupational status, it would appear that unskilled/semi-skilled workers are about only half as likely to have participated as the unemployed, and only two-fifths as likely as skilled workers.

The Swedish report concludes that "the quantitative goals appear to be broadly attainable and the goals themselves correspond fairly closely to the political ambition levels formulated by the government for the next few years". Job related training is seen as a responsibility of the labour market partners. The partners have extensive agreements where the importance of competence development and education is emphasised. In some agreements there are quantitative goals established by the partners. The government has the overall responsibility for the education system but the government and the partners have a joint responsibility for co-operation in the these matters. In August 1998 a governmental working group presented their report on Skills Development in Professional Life. The group proposes that the government, employers' associations and trade union organisations make a three-way agreement entailing that the government stimulates skills development. This stimulation shall lead to a qualitative and quantitative increase in operationally focused skills development for employees. The working group does not here present any proposal for financing but is in full agreement that responsible financing is an unconditional prerequisite for a stimulation fund being implemented.

Expenditure gaps

Calculation of expenditure gaps, or the additional resources needed to meet targets for lifelong learning, depends on reliable estimates of participation gaps and unit costs for various lifelong learning opportunities. As seen in the preceding discussion, precise estimates are impossible. The cost estimates should be viewed with

© OECD 2000

caution as well. Though they typically are based on historical costs in different sectors, they should be viewed as rough proxies (at best) for a number of reasons. They are average, not marginal costs; thus they do not necessarily give a true indication of costs of adding enrolments in higher education, for example. Marginal costs may be markedly lower if economies of scale are at work, in some forms of distance education for example, or markedly higher if the target population has harder-to-meet needs. The costs sometimes are really outlays per participants (or some other unit), rather than indications of true costs; this results from budget processes in which allocations are not made solely on the basis of expected numbers of persons to be served.

The reports vary in the extent of their coverage of different "sectors" of lifelong learning, and to which they were able to quantify participation gaps, unit costs, and total public resource requirements. They also vary with regard to whether they used OECD targets, or targets that reflected more national circumstances and priorities. Annex 3 summarises the cost estimates. The reader should keep in mind that the participation targets and cost estimates do not necessarily reflect agreed-upon policies. Rather they are intended to indicate the direction and rough magnitudes of resource requirements under particular conditions and assumptions.

Overall, data suggest that:

– For most countries, the objectives/targets and costs estimates used in the analysis are provided for the purpose of illustrating possible policy and cost scenarios; they usually do not reflect agreed upon policy or results from precise estimates of average or marginal cost. The targets of Norway and Finland, for example, reflect policies that are in place or being implemented; those of the Netherlands take fuller account than the original OECD estimates of institutional arrangements, but do not always reflect actual policy. The Czech Republic and Hungary follow the original OECD targets more closely, to demonstrate that the lifelong learning objectives are indeed ambitious and that priorities are needed.

– Countries vary in the extent of the coverage of their estimates. Most do not provide much information on costs associated with expanded pre-school opportunities for young children. More provide estimates for adults; but they are less complete than for estimates related to the formal education system, covering only part of the adult population (Japan, for example), or providing no information on costs (Korea).

– The total cost calculations suggest that, given the targets that countries specify, countries vary considerably in the extent to which the goals of lifelong learning are achievable. No matter how the targets may be defined, the Nordic countries seem closest. The resource requirements appear to be minimal or within reach. In contrast, both the Czech Republic and Hungary, though

Goals, Objectives, and Priorities

specifying different objectives, appear to face substantial resource requirements that force prioritisation.

- The countries that have attempted to provide information on non-public costs – Hungary and Norway – suggest that such costs are likely to most important with respect to adults.

- More generally, it would appear that the net new resource requirements are likely to be most substantial with respect to adults.

- Finally, data on costs of different learning activities are incomplete, particularly for adults.

In looking at results for individual countries, the Dutch analysis is the most comprehensive. The public cost of closing participation gaps in upper secondary and higher education are estimated at 1.33% of public current expenditure and, for adult education of all kinds, the figure is a further 0.98% of public expenditure. These are large figures, especially for a country such as the Netherlands which already has a well-developed system of lifelong education and training.

Hungary also was able to produce detailed estimates of the additional costs that would be incurred in meeting OECD lifelong education costs is. Huge increases in higher education participation are needed to meet OECD enrolment targets and there is also a substantial task of job-related training and retraining needed to meet the needs of a modern economy. The enrolment gaps to be filled in initial secondary and tertiary education are estimated to require additional expenditure equivalent to 5.5% of public expenditure and post-initial education and training requires an additional 6.7% of public funds. In total, these amount to 4.2% of GDP.

In other reports, there were concerns that no usable targets for lifelong education yet exist. In Austria, for example, although the government favours expansion, "no quantitative aims are established for the expansion of lifelong learning". The study also expresses concern about decline in apprenticeships, although this appears to be balanced by increases in enrolments in secondary technical and vocational schools.

The Japanese report considers that there are few participation gaps in relation to the OECD targets. In relation to the ISCED 3 target, the report maintains that "(…) with over 97% of students advancing to high school, we can say there are no gaps". Likewise, there is no gap in relation to tertiary education, where the "advancement rate is almost 69%". For adult education, the assessment is that "there are no gaps pertaining to basic literacy, as it is nearly universal in Japan". Gaps in retraining for employment and job-related training are not estimated "as that data is unavailable". The only gap identified is in "other adult education" and this is not seen as a responsibility of the state.

© OECD 2000

Conclusions

This chapter has intended to open the discussion of how Member countries are to meet the resource requirements of lifelong learning. It has done this by considering how ambitious or how modest a vision of lifelong learning Member countries are pursuing, specifying the operational objectives that need to be met, and estimating what the resource implications are. In presenting the evidence, the chapter has considered how far Member countries have progressed on a continuum in the policy making process, from broad principles, to clearly specified operational targets.

Member countries share the same broad goals of lifelong learning. But they differ from one another in the degree to which they have made progress in articulating and implementing concrete strategies. They differ with respect to starting points, and relative priorities. In Finland and Sweden, for example, lifelong learning begins with nursery education and extends to all types of adult learning throughout life. Similarly, in Japan, there is an emphasis on a broad holistic view of lifelong learning which starts with foundation education and embraces all forms of formal and informal adult learning. In Japan, the concept of lifelong learning is seen as having the potential to transform the school-centred education system. Other countries, such as Austria and Hungary, have more sharply defined conceptions of lifelong learning which include upper secondary, tertiary and adult vocational education and training, but which do not extend much beyond this.

Besides holding differing views of what lifelong learning is in operational terms, OECD countries have different starting points for the development of policy and objectives. Only five of the countries which have contributed to this study have what may be called a comprehensive national strategy for lifelong learning. Even in these countries, objectives in terms of clear operational targets have either only recently been formulated or are still in the process of formulation. The idea of viewing the education and training system through the lens of lifelong learning is still relatively new. Consequently, national authorities in some countries have difficulty in specifying precise objectives.

Broadly speaking, there appear to be two types of rationale for lifelong learning:

– Those countries where lifelong education is seen as a natural progression from having achieved targets for initial primary, secondary and tertiary education.

– Those countries where initial education has not reached target levels, but where the need to develop a modern economy is so pressing that concentrating simply on the annual inflow of trained young people is insufficient to meet economic and social aspirations.

© OECD 2000

There is considerable overlap and few countries fit entirely into either category, but the categorisation does to some extent help to interpret different approaches to the development of realistic lifelong learning policies.

Overall, the reports paint a picture of countries that recognise the importance of lifelong learning for individuals, for economies and for societies, but which are struggling to come to terms with its institutional implications, and the question of how to make it affordable.

On the basis of the available evidence, meeting basic targets will be expensive in most countries. But very few were able to give plausible estimates of the costs of meeting them. For most, estimating the participation rates necessary to come up to OECD target levels did not prove to be too difficult, but costing them in a consistent way to arrive at global estimates of the increases in public outlays needed to meet the targets proved much more challenging. There is a lack of statistical data for appraising the current situation beyond initial secondary and tertiary education in many countries. Good information is available in most OECD countries on participation rates in initial education and it is improving rapidly for *participation* in adult and continuing education and training. However, usable information on costs, particularly in adult education and work-based training is at best patchy. There is a desire in many countries to set up more rigorously defined databases on lifelong learning and particularly its cost implications.

The following chapters examine how the resource requirements of lifelong learning are being, or could be met. They examine developments and strategies under consideration to strengthen the economic incentives for governmental, as well as non-governmental actors to invest in lifelong learning, and the mechanisms for facilitating those actors to pay now for learning that generates benefits in the future.

© OECD 2000

Chapter 2

Increasing the Cost-effectiveness, Quality and Benefits of Lifelong Learning Opportunities

Introduction

As the previous chapter suggests, achieving the goal of lifelong learning is likely to have important resource implications. Even countries that have already achieved high levels of participation in various sectors of learning – Japan, the Netherlands and Sweden, for example – are concerned about the cost of funding an effective lifelong learning system. There is a recognition by all countries of the need to increase the contribution which employers and individuals make to the cost of lifelong learning. This depends on strengthening the incentives for them to invest in lifelong learning, and ensuring that there are the financing mechanisms that enable them to act on those incentives. This chapter looks at the first of these two challenges.

Strengthening incentives to invest in lifelong learning is the same, essentially, as raising expected rates of return. The more net gain that an individual expects to get out of lifelong learning, the more that individual will be motivated to invest in it.

The OECD Member countries covered by this synthesis are pursuing strategies that act on raising rates of return in two ways: *i)* by reducing costs and increasing cost-effectiveness of the processes by which lifelong learning occurs, and *ii)* by increasing the quality and benefits of the outcomes of lifelong learning. This chapter surveys strategies that are in place and under consideration. It also considers the influence of such measures – particularly those to improve efficiency – on equality of access to lifelong learning opportunities.

Difficulties in addressing cost-effectiveness and quality

Different OECD countries are taking their own particular approaches to tackling these issues. This depends on their specific national context and priorities. Although it is possible to identify general trends emerging across countries, there are a number of difficulties that complicate the analysis.

© OECD 2000

Addressing cost-effectiveness in relation to lifelong learning is complicated because the responsibility for ensuring cost-effective and quality of provision is divided between a number of players:

- In most OECD countries, national and/or regional and local government are primarily responsible for governance and funding compulsory education with parents contributing varying, but always small amounts in terms of items such as learning materials. (The position in Japan, however, is somewhat different because of the significant role of private providers.)
- The responsibility at the upper secondary education level is divided between national government, employers and individuals, with employers often contributing substantial amounts for apprenticeship training and individuals usually contributing least.
- Higher and tertiary education is largely, but not exclusively, funded and controlled by national government in most OECD countries, although the financial contribution of individuals is increasing in many countries as fees and loan schemes are being introduced and there is a rise in the number of private universities.
- Adult learning is the most diverse and complex part of the lifelong learning system in terms of its structure and finance. In most OECD countries, education and training for the unemployed and for those with a low level of qualification is organised and funded by national and/or regional government. Work-based in-service training is largely seen as the responsibility of employers, while other vocational or non-vocational adult education and training is normally funded entirely by the individual herself/himself, or a mix of the employer and the individual or, less frequently, partially by national government.

Another problem is that, in many OECD countries, there is still a paucity of accurate information about the costs of lifelong learning. Most available data on "costs" are based, in fact, on outlays, which are loosely related to *average* cost, but are poor indicators of the *marginal* cost of serving one more person in a particular programme, or starting up a new initiative. The concept of using "output-based" or "performance-based" funding for public formal education provision has only recently been introduced into most of the countries which have contributed to this report. The reports suggest that the previous block grant, "input-based" funding systems did not encourage either detailed accounting or cost effectiveness at the institutional level, because there was no reward for increased efficiency. A move to output-based funding, in itself, is thus seen by many countries as a way of raising awareness about the cost of education and training, and of highlighting the need to make the system more efficient and cost-effective, and identifying areas where cost reductions can be made.

Strategies to improve cost-effectiveness and quality in initial education and training

OECD countries are acting to increase the cost-effectiveness of education and training provision across all sectors through four broad strategies:

- Reducing teaching and personnel costs.
- Co-ordination and rationalisation of the education and training system, including opening up the education system to private providers and thus introducing a limited education and training market.
- Devolving responsibility to the level of the provider.
- Increasing the use of information and communication technology (ICT).

Reducing teaching and personnel costs

The largest component of cost associated with lifelong learning that occurs in formal education settings consists of salaries of teachers, trainers and other key personnel in the education and training system. These costs are increasing as the age profile of the teaching population in many countries rises. Although demographic trends across OECD countries indicate a reduction in the number of young people entering secondary and tertiary education over the next few years, this does not necessarily reduce teaching costs in these sectors in the short term. Teachers in many countries are on permanent contracts and are not necessarily easily deployed into other sectors of the education and training system where participation is rising (*e.g.* adult education). Teaching and personnel costs on their own are significantly greater, in most cases, than all other costs put together. It is hardly surprising, therefore, that one of the most important considerations for most countries, when they are looking at how to increase the cost-effectiveness of their current education and training systems, is how to reduce teaching costs.

OECD countries are pursuing a number of strategies to achieve savings in this area. Hungary for example, is increasing the ratio of students to teaching staff in all sectors, including adult basic education. Italy is undertaking a major restructuring of the schools system which involves reducing the number of teachers it employs and increasing student/teacher ratios. The Netherlands reports sharp increases in student/staff ratios in apprenticeship training over the past few years. In Sweden the large savings within the municipalities during the 1990s have also involved economies in the school sector and the pupil/teacher ratio has increased except in upper secondary and special schools. The Czech Republic is increasing the workload for teachers. In Austria, there has been a reduction in in-service training undertaken in school time; for staff in higher education, there is now a legal basis for employment on flexible contracts. In the Netherlands, attempts have already been made, and will continue to be made in the future, to cut expenditure on "reduced pay", the cost of sick leave and disability for staff in all sectors of education. In many countries, notably Hungary, Japan and Norway, introducing distance learning measures and increasing the use of ICT are also seen as ways of decreasing teacher costs. In addition, Japan considers the increased use of teaching assistants at universities, rather than fully qualified teaching staff, as an important way of reducing teaching costs.

However, there is a tension here, which is brought out clearly in the Dutch report, between efficiency measures which have a directly detrimental effect on teachers' conditions of service and the need to retain the type of high quality teaching force required for an effective lifelong learning system. Many countries are already finding it more difficult to attract and retain younger teaching staff who can often get better salaries in other occupations. There is a balance to be struck, therefore, between reducing the level of expenditure on teachers and other education personnel and enhancing the quality of lifelong learning opportunities in order to encourage more people to participate, to achieve and to progress effectively.

Co-ordination and rationalisation of the education and training system

In the majority of OECD countries contributing to this report, there is a recognition that developing a strategy for lifelong learning depends on policies which go beyond the traditional boundaries of Ministries of Education. In Japan, for example, the Ministry of Education, Science, Sports and Culture works with the Ministry of Labour, the Ministry of Health and Welfare, the Ministry of Construction and the Ministry of International Trade and Industry on joint research surveys to foster the development and dissemination of various aspects of lifelong learning. Similarly, there is an increasing focus on the co-ordination of policies being pursued by national government and regional and local authorities in the area of lifelong learning. This level of co-ordination not only provides OECD countries with the kind of strategic overview required for developing lifelong learning systems, but also allows them to look at efficiency measures from a whole-system perspective. Co-operation also extends to partnerships between the public and private sectors.

Co-operation between sectors

In Italy, the *Formazione Tecnico-professionale Superiore* provides a highly integrated approach to lifelong learning through a consortium of secondary schools, universities, professional training centres and enterprises in a particular region. The consortium uses resources made available by the European Union, the state, the region, local authorities and public and private bodies to develop a strong regional link between employment, education, training and professional development. The consortium is thus in the position to respond quickly and flexibly to current and future economic and technological conditions in a particular region.

© OECD 2000

In Austria, since the early 1980s, there has been a development plan for a co-operative system of adult education and training which, among other objectives, has been designed to make more rational use of the available resources by means of co-operation between adult education and other educational institutions, especially with schools. This has been successful to some extent in creating a more co-ordinated approach to adult education and training, particularly greater co-operation between adult education providers and other fields of education.

In 1996, the Netherlands introduced the Adult and Vocational Education Act which set up Regional Education Centres (ROCs). These centres are the responsibility of the Ministry of Education, but have considerable autonomy. They have been formed through the merger of institutions involved in the delivery of secondary vocational education, apprenticeship and adult education and have resulted both in a more flexible delivery service and in savings through more efficient use of accommodation and educational resources.

Qualifications frameworks

Qualifications frameworks provide another means for improving co-operation between sectors insofar as they make it easier for individuals to have skills and competence acquired in one sector, recognised in another. Austria, Denmark, Hungary, Italy, the Netherlands and Norway, are currently focusing attention on the development of more unified and common qualifications systems that facilitate credit accumulation and transfer across different sectors of the education and training system. This work is seen as providing the basis for making their education and training systems more transparent to learners and to end users such as employers. Moreover, it is recognised that a country's qualifications system should reflect the move towards lifelong learning if participation in education and training throughout life is to be valued and the education and training system is to be seen as a coherent whole.

Rationalisation

Alongside these moves for greater co-ordination and coherence in terms of countries' education and training systems, there is also a strong trend towards rationalisation. As a result of demographic trends, many countries are looking to rationalise their compulsory and upper secondary education systems in order to increase the amount of public funding available for other parts of the education and training system. The Netherlands, for example, has been involved in what it describes as a "merger wave", which started in 1990. Since that date, a number of general secondary schools have merged with other schools to form larger comprehensive schools. This is intended to ensure that accommodation and equipment are used in a more efficient way so as to reduce the capital expenditure on secondary education. Italy is also in the process of

© OECD 2000

restructuring and rationalising its whole secondary education system which has already resulted in a considerable reduction in overall staffing costs. Hungary is planning to make similar moves in relation to university courses and institutions. It is felt that larger more comprehensive higher education institutions will be much more cost effective than the current system of small, scattered and often specialist institutions. Rationalisation also extends to strategies to consolidate resources within sectors. In Sweden, for example, schools are reducing the range of courses and programmes on offer. In Austria, schools are reducing the number of lessons in some curriculum areas and limiting expenditure on textbooks. In the Czech Republic, authorities increasing the amount of short-course foundation provision for adults in schools as a way of raising revenue for these schools.

In the tertiary education area, there is a focus in OECD countries on modernising the type of provision on offer in higher education institutions to make it both more flexible and responsive and, potentially, more cost-effective. The Czech Republic, the Netherlands and Sweden, for example, are focusing on the length of student programmes and are considering setting a fixed length of study time for degrees. In addition, Austria and the Netherlands are rationalising the number and type of courses on offer and, in some cases, the number of institutions where particular courses may be offered. Many OECD countries are also introducing changes to the type of provision they offer in higher education institutions to increase efficiency. Hungary, for example is looking to increase short course provision; Austria is improving the flexibility and speed of the processes required for the introduction of new courses to meet modern needs; and both Austria and Hungary are increasingly introducing modular and individually tailored student programmes.

There is wide recognition that high drop-out rates are costly in the short term because they waste the efforts of students and institutional capacity; over the longer term they are seen as detrimental to future participation in lifelong learning. It is believed that in order to ensure student retention and achievement, there is need to make provision more attractive and relevant in order to increase student participation. To this end, Austria has introduced an induction period for university students which has helped to increase retention and to prevent so many costly course changes. Italy has generalised the *numerus clausus* for enrolment and the Netherlands has laid a greater emphasis on the selection and referral of students in the first phase of higher education to avoid high drop out rates.

Finally, within the framework of lifelong learning, perhaps the most vital agent for rationalisation is the learner himself. Indeed, an important element of lifelong learning is ensuring that learners are adequately prepared to manage their own learning: learning to know what is needed and when, and where learning opportunities can be found or created. Though this transition from learning strategies and opportunities being defined by institutions, to being defined by individuals appears to be still

© OECD 2000

> Box 2.1. **The Study House Initiative in the Netherlands**
>
> The purpose of the Study House is to promote active and autonomous learning and to provide learners with broader programmes which recognise their individual interests, strengths and weaknesses. The programmes on offer are designed to make progression from secondary and tertiary education easier and more effective by introducing four broad connective themes which relate to everyday life – technical science, economics and society, nature and health and nature and technical science. The connections between and within these different subjects will be made explicit to learners so that they are more able to link what they learn in secondary education with new subjects or areas of knowledge introduced in tertiary education. These four broad connective themes have also been designed to give learners access to a wide range of tertiary education institutions. In addition, learners are involved in activities which promote active and independent learning and team work and are given careers education and guidance to ensure not only that they are aware of all the options open to them at the end of compulsory schooling, but also that they have developed the knowledge and skills to make the most effective use of these opportunities.

relatively rare, the *Studiehuis* (Study House) Initiative in the Netherlands offers one example of how a country is dealing with this issue (Box 2.1).

Competition

Finally, many OECD countries are relying on expanded private capacity and increased competition in the provision of learning opportunities. This is seen as a way to improve efficiency in the education and training system, and to allow increased capacity to meet the rising demand for lifelong learning. Japan has relied on private providers in all sectors of the education and training for some time and recognises that the rapid expansion of participation in higher education could not have been achieved without this type of provision. Hungary and the Czech Republic have both passed legislation (in 1990 and 1998, respectively) to allow the establishment of private universities. The purpose in doing so was to help generate new capacity and encourage cost-effectiveness. The Danish Ministry of Labour relies entirely on outside providers for the provision of all its training and learning opportunities. Half are purchased from adult education providers supported by the Ministry of Education; the rest are purchased from technical/commercial colleges and business schools. Outcomes are certificated in the same way, regardless of provider. In Austria, authorities are developing a form of accreditation for local and foreign private institutions of higher education as a means of increasing the scope and scale of opportunities.

© OECD 2000

Devolving responsibility to the level of the provider

Funding mechanisms, funding levers and incentives are increasingly being used to encourage both efficiency and quality of the education and training systems in OECD countries. Alongside the strategies for co-ordination and rationalisation of education and training systems at the national and regional level described above, the majority of OECD countries are also moving towards devolving responsibility for budgetary decisions to the institutional level. Funding on the basis of outcomes rather than inputs (as in the Danish taximeter scheme), leaves institutions free to decide how to achieve learning outcomes. This is designed to increase institutional autonomy in two ways. First, devolving responsibility is seen as a means of encouraging efficient use of budgets. Secondly, it is hoped that this initiative will introduce incentives for institutions to market their services for their own profit. Devolving responsibility for financial accountably to the level of the education or training provider is seen as particularly effective when it is combined with more sophisticated forms of accounting, such as output-based cost measures, which heighten the provider's awareness of the costs of education. It is argued that when this responsibility and knowledge remains at the level of national government departments or regional or local agencies, there is little incentive for individual providers to reduce their expenditure or manage resources efficiently.

The Finnish country report provides one example of how funding decisions are being devolved to the institutional level (Box 2.2).

However, as a later part of this chapter indicates, there is a need to ensure that both quality and equity issues are not sacrificed to efficiency when education and training providers are given more autonomy over their budgets. OECD countries are clearly aware of this danger and some of the measures they are taking at the national level, in order to balance the greater autonomy at institutional level, are discussed in later parts of this chapter.

The use of ICT for increasing efficiency and cost-effectiveness

ICT is seen by many OECD countries as one of the most effective ways of increasing and widening participation in lifelong learning while keeping down costs to an affordable level. Japan, in particular, stresses the importance of this particular solution to its vision of a learning society where all have access to lifelong learning. It also provides a number of examples of how it is addressing this issue in all sectors, but particularly in higher and adult education. Notable initiatives include the development of the "University of the Air" which began to enrol students in 1985 and now has a student population of approximately 62 000. It uses correspondence, satellites and ground circuits to provide joint conferences and classes among different education providers. There is a similar initiative in Korea called the Korean National Open University (Box 2.3).

Box 2.2. **State subsidy system for education in Finland**

The essential characteristics of the Finnish state subsidy system for compulsory comprehensive schools, upper secondary schools and initial vocational education, as well as education leading to a degree at a polytechnic and long-term specialisation programmes at the polytechnics, are as follows.

Unit costs are determined in advance for the following year; decisions concerning the arrangements and financing of education by a municipality or another owner of an institution which receives funding during the fiscal year do not influence unit costs. If a recipient is able to organise education at a lower price than that of the unit costs, its state subsidy will not decrease. On the other hand, if the actual expenditure exceeds the level of unit costs, the recipient will be solely responsible for these expenses. Therefore, the system encourages cost-effectiveness among providers of educational services.

In a financing system based on unit costs, the use of the funds granted are not tied to specific conditions for granting and calculating these funds, which enable municipalities and other providers of services to make independent decisions when allocating funds for various purposes. Primarily, this means that the recipient can decide on the allocation of resources within the educational system. On the other hand, the law does not prohibit the use of unit cost funding for purposes other than education. It has been feared that this will lead, especially in the municipalities, to the allocation of funds granted for education to other services provided by the municipality, such as social welfare and health care. However, in practice, it is not possible to run an educational institution on state funding alone without additional funding allocated by the provider of the services, especially the municipalities.

The system's administration is not as heavy as that of the state subsidy system which was in use earlier because institutions and other providers of education do not need to compile reports on how the state subsidy funds have been used, nor do these reports have to be dealt with by state authorities. This clearly reduces administrative costs.

Moreover, all unit costs have been cut since 1993 due to savings procedures put in place to balance the budget in Finland. Therefore the unit costs do not in practice equal the average total national expenses. This has enhanced the cost-effectiveness element included in the unit cost system. On the other hand, the responsibility of the owners of education institutions, particularly the municipalities, has grown in comparison with central government.

The unit cost system encourages the municipalities and other providers of educational services to act economically. Unit costs are calculated once every two years according to actual educational expenditure. If the average expenses for education decrease, so will the unit costs and the state subsidy. Therefore, it is also in the state's interest to see the municipalities and other providers of educational services perform economically. The system thus has an in-built mechanism for lowering unit costs. Cuts made to balance the budget have strengthened this element.

> **Box 2.3. Korean National Open University (KNOU)**
>
> KNOU was established in 1972 and now enrols well over 200 000 students. 177 000 students have graduated since its inception. It is thus the largest single provider of higher education in Korea.
>
> Admission to KNOU is open to adults as well as to high school graduates and its primary mission is to provide lifelong education by departing from the restrictions of conventional methods of instruction. It is not only organised in a different way from traditional higher education institutions, but also makes use of advanced distance education systems such as cable TV, video-conferencing and the VOD system satellite network.
>
> KNOU has thus shown the potential of ICT for teaching and learning in tertiary education. KNOU is recognised for its contribution in helping to fulfil the enormous demand for higher education from working adults. It also pursues efficient and cost-effective approaches to programme delivery and management. But the most important role KNOU fulfils is in its mission of offering additional lifelong learning opportunities for disadvantaged adults.

Sweden's Forestry Project Initiative (Box 2.4), designed to address employers' needs for a more highly educated workforce, provides an example of how ICT is being used to increase cost-effectiveness in the adult education sector. The study programme offered is considered to be more attractive than institutionally-based teaching programmes to potential participants, because they do not have to bear the costs of foregone earnings or accommodation costs often associated with more conventional educational provision. In addition, the contribution of the employers is lower than with conventional provision because they do not have to bear the cost of production losses. There is thus a greater incentive for both employees and employers to invest in this type of education.

The Norwegian Network with Information Technology Project (Box 2.5) is another example of a cost-effective experiment with ICT. In 1998, approximately 2 000 students participated in this type of open and flexible learning environment each semester.

OECD countries are beginning to experiment with ICT solutions to increase the cost-effectiveness of lifelong learning provision and see these experiments as an important part of their strategy for building lifelong learning systems. At the same time, project initiators stress that ICT also can be used to increase and widen participation in lifelong learning and can thus address some of the equity issues which underpin the vision of lifelong learning in many countries.

© OECD 2000

> Box 2.4. **Forestry Project Initiative in Sweden**
>
> The aim of this project is to provide shift workers in the forestry industry with upper secondary level education in the core subjects of mathematics, chemistry, physics, Swedish and English. Tuition is carried out mainly through distance education and with the support of supervisors and new technology such as computers and interactive video. Education takes place mainly outside working hours, but in close proximity to learners' homes or workplaces.
>
> Paper and pulp is a processing industry with production methods that are highly computerised and automated. Working as an operator imposes great demands on technical knowledge. Companies have great difficulty in recruiting personnel with a three-year upper secondary education, which in practice is the lowest theoretical educational background needed to manage the technology of the manufacturing process. Employees must also have good basic knowledge to acquire the necessary competence and technical education. By educating existing personnel in core subjects at the upper secondary level, the companies solve the problem of obtaining personnel with sufficient basic knowledge, at the same time as retaining the skills their employees already have.
>
> Employees in the paper and pulp industry work shifts and have working hours which make it impossible for them to carry out part-time studies in traditional adult education. Socio-economic factors also make it more difficult for them to stay away from work and family too long. Moreover, longer absence from work would result in the loss of their current skills. This project is designed to address all these issues.
>
> In January 1998, 12 paper mills were participating in the project and 231 employees were taking part. These mills are located all over Sweden and are typical of the industry in terms of capacity and number of employees. The project is managed by a steering group made up of a representative from the educational organisers, the employers and the industry's trade union.
>
> The type of partnership approach between government, employers and individual learners, which is seen as the way forward for lifelong learning in many countries, is evident in this project. The employers take responsibility for providing suitable premises for learning centres equipped with the necessary ICT close to their factories. They are also responsible for paying supervisors. For its part, the government has granted SEK 1.4m per year over the three years of the project. The employees' side of the bargain is to be prepared to study outside working hours.

However, although ICT is seen as a potential way of increasing the cost-effectiveness of education and training systems in the longer run, there are two major problems for some OECD countries in the shorter term. The first is that the initial start-up and infrastructure costs will be high in those countries which have not heavily

> Box 2.5. **The Norwegian Network with Information Technology (NITOL Project) in Norway**
>
> All Norwegian universities and colleges are connected through an electronic infrastructure. Some of the universities and colleges are now co-operating to offer students on and off campus electronic access to lessons given at these institutions via the Internet. By combining the use of relatively inexpensive equipment such as video cameras and computers in the classroom, students outside the campus have access to lessons simultaneously with students on campus. This allows for flexible access to tuition both by students and teachers – the student can access a lesson when it suits her/his timetable and the teacher can integrate the lessons of others into her/his own courses. The institutions currently participating in this project have agreed a on contract for co-operation, including the sharing of learning materials. In addition, electronic conferences are set up for communication between teachers, students and tutors, so that seminars, discussion groups and the setting and marking of assignments can be carried out in a more flexible and cost-effective manner. In a two-week period, for example, tutors taking part in this project were able to answer 2 000 questions from 570 students. To date, approximately 2 000 students have participated in this type of open and flexible learning environment each semester. About 90 different courses will be offered in open and flexible learning mode. These courses cost on average about one fifth of more conventional courses, depending on the amount of preparation, guidance and follow up work required, and are thus considered very cost-effective.

invested in ICT to date. However, falling costs and increased flexibility in the technology are reducing the importance of start up costs as a barrier to wider ICT use. A second, more stubborn barrier is a lack of expertise among teaching and other education personnel in some countries.

Tertiary education

Improving cost-effectiveness and quality for adult learners

A considerable amount of learning opportunities for adults are found in adult education and training programmes operated by ministries of education; often they exist side by side with the initial education. But a substantial share of learning opportunities for adults – more than a majority of such opportunities by some estimates (OECD, 1997), are found in settings that are far more diffuse than for younger persons.

They range from self-improvement or leisure education, to labour market training for the unemployed and other special groups, to community-based learning activities, to enterprise-based training, both formal and informal. Though there is wide recognition in the country reports that adult learning is a key area for lifelong learning, it is less straightforward than initial education and training, for public authorities to improve cost-effectiveness and quality. Adult learning is mixed frequently with other activities (work, job search), often is financed from non-public resources (individuals and employers), and often is found in settings (the workplace, community, and home) beyond the reach of customary education and training policies.

For adult learning that occurs in programmes and institutions operated by ministries of education, one can find the same kind of measures as those discussed above for improving efficiency and quality in initial education. Such strategies sometimes build on establishing closer relationships between public providers and companies. In Austria, for example, there is a focus on co-operation between the public education sector and private adult education and training organisations to make mutual savings on the development costs of new forms of study. Here, as in the tertiary sector, several countries are also looking at cost-cutting strategies for publicly funded adult education and training. These include, for example, improving the transition from compulsory to supplementary and specialist education (*e.g.* Sweden), and developing more flexible learning programmes for adult learners through the introduction of shorter and more intensive courses with a greater number of starting points in the year (*e.g.* Hungary, the Netherlands and Sweden). There is also great interest in many countries in the development of more effective forms of pedagogy, particularly those which make use of ICT.

One of the complications arising for adults in lifelong learning is having know-how and knowledge acquired in different settings evaluated and recognised. The problem does not exist where adults return to a formal education system and enrol in an education programme that leads to the next higher qualification. Problems may arise, however, when adults wish to get some credit for the know-how and knowledge that they have acquired through experience. Insofar as such experience is not counted, it devalues work based learning relative to academic learning, while also increasing the cost of learning for adults by requiring them to expend time and money to relearn in an academic setting what they already know. Many OECD countries have had in place for years programmes for the assessment of prior learning that are intended to allow adults to enrol in education on the basis of what they know, not just on the basis of the highest previous educational qualification. The emphasis on lifelong learning is leading some countries to encourage wider use and strengthening of these approaches. In Norway, adults have a right to have their non-formal learning evaluated and recognised. Typically this is accomplished by sitting trade examinations; those who pass can have the resulting qualification recognised

© OECD 2000

in the workplace, as well as by education institutions. As wider use of this approach has been encouraged, the number of persons taking advantage of the scheme has grown rapidly. The 1998 White Paper on Competence Reform provides the basis for more systematic recognition of non-formal learning. In Denmark, the Ministry of Labour's main training programmes lead to certificated outcomes. In contrast, the Ministry of Education in the past has paid little attention to recognition of adult learning except insofar as it has been part of normal degree programmes. However, new initiatives are intended to provide a framework that allows individuals to have learning in different settings systematically recognised. Part of the purpose in doing so is to reduce the kinds and duration of education and training that individuals pursue. Measures to increase the transparency and portability of qualifications, introduced in the Netherlands and proposed in Finland, have served to make the benefits from training more predictable, thus encouraging more personal investment. Such measures strengthen the incentives for firms to invest in human resource development by facilitating the efficient allocation of the resulting skills, competences and know-how.

Many countries view improved guidance and advice for adults as a potentially cost-effective way of reducing wasteful drop out and non-completion rates, as well as increasing participation in education and training. As with higher education, there is recognition of the importance of strong individual counselling and advice both to encourage adults to participate in lifelong learning and to help them to progress and achieve. Individual action planning, particularly with the unemployed, has been seen as a very effective way of tailoring training more closely to individual needs and combining support and counselling for education and work.

Active labour market policies and training for the unemployed are another important form of publicly supported adult education and training. This is an area where national government cannot work effectively without the support of private enterprises. Two case studies (Box 2.6 and 2.7) demonstrate how this type of partnership between national government and the private sector can be achieved through the devolving of resources to the local level where they can be used to tackle the problems of unemployment swiftly and cost-effectively.

As another strategy, some governments encourage the development of new institutional settings (such as the National Training Fund, in the Czech Republic) as a way of increasing flexibility in administration as well as in teaching and learning approaches. In Japan (Box 2.8), Lifelong Learning Foundations free providers of adult education and training from the kind of constraints which normally inhibit public organisations from attracting private finance and being able to respond flexibly to market demands.

© OECD 2000

Box 2.6. Work Foundations in Austria

Work foundations are a relatively new institution for the labour market in Austria. The first such institution was the "Steel Foundation", which was established in 1987 and is still in existence. It is characterised by a new form of financing of labour market policies and is designed to provide vocational and continuing education and training, as well as re-integrating employees who have been made redundant back into the workplace.

Work foundations do not replace existing forms of training or systems of job placement for the unemployed. They instead combine both of these functions and represent an alternative form of financing and organisation of labour market specific measures. Work foundations are set up in the wake of redundancies at one or more enterprises and are provided by associations, enterprises or local or regional authorities. Their aim is comprehensive support of employees in their re-integration into the world of work.

The initiative for the establishment of work foundations does not come from the Public Employment Service, but from enterprises, works councils, or from employers' and employees' associations which are seeking collaboration with public authorities. The financing of the work foundations is divided between a number of parties, including enterprises, local authorities, *Länder* governments, staff and employers' associations. If those involved agree on a concept and a social plan that offers sufficient safeguarding of financial, organisational, material and personnel-related resources, the Public Employment Service has to recognise the work foundation officially. This means that the participants in the foundation are legally entitled to draw unemployment benefit for the duration of the foundation up to a maximum of four years.

Depending on the target group and particular circumstances, four types of work foundations can be distinguished: enterprise foundations, insolvency foundations, branch foundations and regional foundations. The various services rendered are: support measures for active job search (job application training, surveys on staff requirements and needs in a specific region, placement services), vocational and continuing education and training measures (organisation of specific courses, programmes and in-company placements), and support of company foundations (legal advice, help in the drawing up of a business concept and financial support). Initially, there are activities which are designed to make the redundant employees familiar with their new situation and to provide occupational re-orientation, since the majority of participants will need to move into a new career after a period of long employment.

The new feature of work foundations is the type of financing and support measures for unemployed persons. As far as financing is concerned, the advantages of work foundations lie in the fact that, in addition to the usual resources unemployed persons receive from the Public Employment Service, additional money is raised. This includes funds from enterprises and staff, local authorities and the *Länder* governments, as well as from the resources of the European Social Fund. These additional resources allow work organisations to offer a wide range of measures for the benefit of the participants, thereby increasing their chances for re-entry into working life.

© OECD 2000

Box 2.6. **Work Foundations in Austria** (*cont.*)

For enterprises there is an incentive to join work foundations in that they can demonstrate their commitment to their social responsibility in a particular area, in spite of staff redundancies, thereby counteracting the loss of their reputation in the region. Work foundations ensure a more socially acceptable form of structural change through the use of the comprehensive measures mentioned above and the generous support offered to dismissed employees, thus reducing the probability of industrial disputes. There is a further benefit which must not be overlooked. The establishment of work foundations in which local authorities, *Länder* governments, enterprises and staff participate draws public attention to the problems of the respective enterprises, regions or branches. This counteracts the otherwise widespread tendency to blame those who have been made redundant for their unemployment. This removes a major obstacle in terms of the re-employment of those who have been made redundant.

Another major advantage of work foundations, in comparison with traditional measures for dealing with unemployment, is that each foundation has its own independent management structure. In this way, problems of unemployment are solved in a decentralised manner with less bureaucracy, and there is a shared feeling of responsibility for how the resources of the foundation are used. Measures and programmes can be adapted to the specific needs, requirements and potential of the respective region and of the participants themselves. A greater number of institutions from the region (enterprises, local authorities, branches of local or regional authorities and training institutions) can be involved in the activities of the work foundation and already existing contacts and information can be utilised. Furthermore, the establishment of work foundations facilitates early placement and vocational training which can begin immediately after an employee has been made redundant. Thus, a less painful transition from redundancy to professional re-orientation and re-qualification becomes possible. Finally, but most important, the danger of social isolation is counteracted by bringing together those who have been made redundant in a work foundation and by carrying out joint reorientation activities.

The activities of work foundations are supervised by the Public Employment Service and, normally, by representatives of those institutions which are contributing financially to the foundation. Some work foundation also themselves carry out regular evaluations of the success of the measures they are putting into place.

Despite their success, work foundations face a number of problems related to the variety and the heterogeneous composition of participating institutions. In many cases, conflicts of interest arise between regional politicians, trade unions, and companies which are not participating in the work foundation. In addition, since providers and financial backers of work foundations are not identical, there can also be conflicts of interest in this respect. A good foundation management is of greatest importance for handling such conflicts and making the work foundation successful.

> Box 2.6. **Work Foundations in Austria** (*cont.*)
>
> In the period between 1987 and the end of 1997, approximately 80 work foundations were running in Austria. To take 1995 as an example, there were 52 work foundations: two branch foundations, 10 insolvency foundations, 16 regional foundations, and 24 enterprise foundations. In these 52 foundations, assistance was provided for 3 709 people, of whom men constituted 64% of the total. 1 898 people completed their foundation measures and slightly more than 70% found a job. In 1995, the Public Employment Service spent a total of ATS 229.2 million on training and unemployment benefit and ATS 103.7 million on additional measures within the framework of work foundations. There is no available information about the expenses of work foundations over and above those paid by the Public Employment Service.

Other measures to improve the quality of lifelong learning opportunities

High quality education and training is more likely to encourage learners to participate and employers to appreciate the benefits for their enterprises of lifelong learning. It is suggested, therefore, that both learners and employers will have a greater incentive to invest in lifelong learning, if it is considered not only efficient, but also if it is of high quality. It could be argued that some of the efficiency measures described earlier in this chapter might have a negative effect on the quality of lifelong learning opportunities, since they stress the importance of reducing costs. However, in the majority of the OECD country reports increasing efficiency is not seen as a zero sum game in relation to quality. In several countries, funding methodologies are being developed which are intended to have an effect on both efficiency and quality. Denmark, Finland, Hungary, the Netherlands and Sweden, for example, are experimenting with output-related funding for their education and training systems. In the case of Finland and the Netherlands, student benefits are increasingly tied to satisfactory study outcomes, so that both institutions and individuals are being incentivised to increase the cost-effectiveness of the education and training system. Though the reports from Austria and Italy raise the possibility that funding follow the student, thereby allowing students to choose which institution to attend according to the quality and flexibility of provision, Denmark is the only country in which such a funding mechanism is actually used.

Just as more autonomy is being given to institutions for financial management, so a similar move is taking place in relation to quality – the responsibility is increasingly being devolved down to the institutional level, although always within clearly defined national parameters. Despite these types of safeguards, however, there still

Box 2.7. **The Adult Education Initiative in Sweden**

The Adult Education Initiative is a five-year investment in adult education that started on July 1st 1997 and is intended to halve unemployment by the year 2000. In the first instance, it will not only increase the scope of upper secondary school education, but it will also shape adult education to the changing individual, working life and societal demands of the next millennium. The investment involves the creation of more than 100 000 new places in adult education annually. Additionnally, there are 10 000 places in folk high school education, 5 000 places in municipal adult education at the compulsory level and 5 000 places in pilot projects for advanced vocational training. When fully implemented, the initiative will provide 140 000 places annually, which corresponds to 3.5% of the total labour force.

Adults who have the greatest need for education and who have so far received least in terms of educational resources, will have the opportunity to develop new knowledge and skills. The main target group for the Adult Education Initiative is, in the first instance, those who are unemployed and either completely, or partially, lack a three-year upper secondary school qualification, but it also focuses on the needs of employees with little post-compulsory education or training. This initiative is particularly aimed at those who are in occupations and industries which are being adversely affected by the market and structural changes (*e.g.* offices, health care and manufacturing industry).

This client group will have access to educational opportunities rather than unemployment benefits in the first instance. Within the framework of the Adult Education Initiative, opportunities for co-operation and joint utilisation of resources at the national employment offices and municipalities will be improved. This initiative will not replace existing education, but instead provide an additional opportunity for adults to acquire education at the same time as other educational alternatives are also open to them. Not only the volume, but also the content of courses will vary and the training will be carried out by different education providers under the overall planning and organisation of the municipalities.

Municipalities have thus been allocated a new role as co-ordinators and have been made responsible for creating an infrastructure for adult education, but not necessarily for organising all the education. They can choose between offering the education themselves or together with other educational organisers and local enterprises. For this reason, emphasis is put on the need to co-operate with Study Associations, Trade Unions, Folk High Schools, the Vocational Training Centre and private educational organisers. With the exception of education provided by folk high schools, the syllabi and grading criteria in municipal adult education will apply regardless of the provider, so that a degree of central control over quality is maintained.

A number of municipalities have already set up "knowledge centres" with personnel from both the employment office and the municipality, where other education providers also have the opportunity to work together under a single structure.

© OECD 2000

Box 2.7. **The Adult Education Initiative in Sweden** (*cont.*)

Individual learners' desires, needs and circumstances will be instrumental in steering and shaping the form and content of the activity. Municipal adult education's traditional content of general theoretical subjects is supplemented by a major increase in vocational courses. Theory and practice are woven together into a new form of workplace training for adults. Different modes of study are available with increased use of distance education, part-time studies, evening course, and study sessions during the school holidays. One-year intensive preparatory course for higher education are also available.

A total of SEK 5 billion has been allocated to the municipalities from central government for this initiative. These funds can be allocated by the municipality in the way which best suits their local circumstances. However, municipalities have to demonstrate how they have produced the number of places for which they bid and how they have met the quality measures they have described in their application for funding. There is also an expectation that municipalities will participate in a monitoring and evaluation exercise. A pre-condition for the state grant to be paid out is that municipalities maintain the volume of upper secondary school education which they finance.

Box 2.8. **The Lifelong Learning Foundation in Kameoka, Japan**

The Lifelong Learning Foundation in Kameoka was established in 1990 to promote all types of adult education with the support of local enterprises. The foundation is an independent institution which is not controlled by the Board of Education or local government but is closely associated with the mayor's office. Kameoka gave its Lifelong Learning Foundation 50 million yen as start-up costs. It was intended that donations would then be collected from citizens, local groups and corporations to reach the target of 2 billion yen. In the event, this amount of money was not fully realised, but enough was available to set up a number of innovative lifelong learning projects and projects promoting internationalism. In addition, some of the funding was used to provide grants for lifelong learning. The foundation publishes a newsletter twice a year to publicise its activities and to promote lifelong learning. The fact that the foundation is a private organisation allows it to collect funding in a way that is not possible for public organisations. The foundation's board also has a large degree of autonomy over what kind of activities it supports in its own locality and can thus tailor its programmes to serve the needs of its citizens more effectively.

remains a concern in some countries, such as the Netherlands, that the funding models it uses for some sectors do not include sufficient incentives to improve the quality of education. The response here, as in other countries which share this concern, is to increase the strength and importance of other internal and external mechanisms to monitor quality.

The system used in the Netherlands (Box 2.9) for its tertiary education system provides a useful example of this mixed approach to quality assurance.

Box 2.9. **Quality and Study Ease Programme in the Netherlands**

According to the "Quality and Study Ease" Bill which was passed in 1996, all institutions of higher education must guarantee their students that they can complete their study within the formal duration of the course. If the students are unable to finish their study within the duration of the study period because of barriers caused by the institutions, the students can hold the institutions responsible for the extra costs they have incurred. Mutual obligations for institutions and students are laid down in the "Student By-Laws, New Style" which all students receive when they enter higher education.

In addition to this financial incentive, higher education institutions in the Netherlands have to develop a quality management plan which is based on an internal evaluation of the functioning of the institution and sets down priorities for the improvement of courses and proposals for meeting these. Without a quality management plan, institutions have no right to draw money from the "Study Ease Enabling Fund". These plans are appraised by an independent external committee which advises the Minister of Education, Culture and Science on the proposals for improving quality and introducing innovative practice. The institutions must then issue a report on the results of developments, as outlined in their plan, to ensure that money is spent appropriately.

The discussion below examines in more detail of role of government and providers in improving quality assurance in learning settings.

The role of national government in quality assurance

As has been indicated above, OECD countries still see national governments as having an important role in quality assurance, despite, or even because of, the increasing trend to devolve responsibility for delivery of education and training to the institutional level. In a few countries, such as Hungary and Sweden, one body has jurisdiction for quality assurance across all public education and training sectors. In others, there are different agencies for the different sectors. In the Czech Republic there is a Certifications Committee for higher education, an Accreditation Committee for retraining the unemployed and an Evaluation Programme for higher vocational schools. The individual country reports suggest that, despite their different national systems, national governments play a role in assuring and improving quality in three ways – building the infrastructure for a system of lifelong learning, developing the human resource base required to improve the education and training system and assuring the quality of education and training provision at the point of delivery. Each of these is discussed below.

Building the infrastructure for a system of lifelong learning

There are a number of areas where national government, in some cases in conjunction with the social partners, is ideally situated to build the infrastructure for a system of lifelong learning. Six such areas are considered here.

First, it is only national government with the social partners which is able to validate, and in some cases, develop a nationally recognised system for assessment and evaluation of skills and competences, and credit accumulation and transfer system. The development of such a system is seen as of paramount importance in assuring quality in adult education in Hungary and the Netherlands, for example, as well as ensuring that learning is adequately assessed and signalled, regardless of whether it occurs in a formal education setting. In Austria there is a strong emphasis on using such an approach to assure quality in secondary education, in particular. Similarly in the Czech Republic, Japan and Korea there are strong arguments for certification for adult education and training which are recognised across different sectors. In the latter country, not only does certification indicate a person's competence in relation to a particular set of skills or body of knowledge, but also, in some cases, entitles the holder to financial remuneration. It is therefore essential that common standards pertain for all education and training providers. This is an area which the Netherlands is focusing on through the development of a national qualifications structure for vocational education.

A second role for national government is to ensure that transparent and effective progression routes exist in and between different parts of the lifelong learning system. Currently there is a focus in Austria, for example, on the quality of apprenticeship and technical vocational training and, more particularly, on the amount of general education such programmes contain, in order to ensure that learners on these programmes have access to higher education. Similarly, the Netherlands is looking closely at the links between foundation and tertiary education and senior and higher vocational education to ensure that clear progression routes are open to learners.

Third, national government is seen as having a role in ensuring that funding mechanisms build in elements to assure high quality education provision and a minimum

© OECD 2000

student entitlement, as well as efficiency. There are two major ways in which OECD national governments are tackling this issue. First, there is a trend towards national government and education and training providers jointly setting and monitoring targets and outcomes to be met by the providers. Second, there is, as we have seen above, an increasing move to link financial incentives to the quality and innovation of delivery.

A fourth role for national government in assuring the quality of lifelong learning opportunities is by collecting (and in some cases publishing) national statistics on achievement and progression, as well as enrolment. This not only potentially improves the quality of student decision-making, and thus helps to stimulate a market in education and training, but also focuses institutions on student retention and achievement rates as well as on initial recruitment.

Fifth, many OECD countries see national government as having a role in stipulating minimum requirements for courses and certain types of training such as apprenticeships.

Finally, many OECD countries wish national government to play a major role in building up the national infrastructure of ICT and for assuring the quality of this type of provision.

Developing the human resource base required to improve the education and training system

There are three major ways in which OECD countries see national government having a role to play in developing the human resource base required to improve the quality of the education and training system. The first is to lay down minimum qualification requirements for teachers and instructors involved in all sectors of the lifelong education and training system. The second is to introduce better management training and qualifications for those in charge of publicly funded institutions. The third is to set up ICT training for all teachers and instructors involved in the education and training system.

Assuring the quality of education and training provision at the point of delivery

The role of national government in assuring the quality of education and training provision at the point of delivery has been discussed to some degree earlier in this chapter. However, it might be useful to return to this issue here, because of the concern which many OECD countries share that the focus both on privatisation and on efficiency measures might have a detrimental effect on the quality of their education and training provision.

There appears, for example, to be an anxiety in some countries about the role of private training providers in adult education and training because of the possibility that they might compromise quality to low costs. The reports from Austria and Finland therefore argue strongly for the continuation of publicly subsidised continuing education and training, which has a strong involvement by employers, employees and trade unions, but where the content and quality of the programmes remains the responsibility of national or regional providers of education. Moreover, as the Austrian report points out, this also ensures that learning programmes in the workplace and in formal education institutions are complementary, thereby ensuring clear progression routes between the two and thus facilitating lifelong learning. However, in the Dutch system, although private providers offer vocational qualifications and award diplomas, central government retains responsibility for quality. A further area where several OECD countries feel that national government has an important role to play is in setting up centres of excellence in relation to particular sectors or specific teaching and learning methodologies. The report from the Netherlands cites two examples of centres for disseminating good practice: the Consortium for Innovation in Higher Education, and the Centre for Educational Innovation in Vocational and Adult Education (CINOP) (Box 2.10).

Box 2.10. **The Consortium for Innovation in Higher Education in the Netherlands**

The Open University, in conjunction with twelve universities and institutes for higher and vocational education in the Netherlands and Flanders, established the Consortium for Innovation in Higher Education in 1996. The consortium works on a project basis and non-members can join occasional projects. Partners have to bring in their own budget and capacity. The aim of the consortium is to contribute to innovation in higher education by systematically using ICT. Projects either lead to practical applications of ICT in educational practice or to applied research into the possibilities of using ICT in education and training. The advantage of the latter type of project is that universities are encouraged to pool their resources which helps to ensure that unnecessary duplication of work can be avoided and that solutions are reached in the most cost-effective way and to the benefit of the whole sector.

The Centre for Educational Innovation in Vocational and Adult Education in the Netherlands

The Centre for Educational Innovation in Vocational and Adult Education (CINOP) supports educational institutions with research and development in vocational and adult education. Its most important goal is to enhance the link between education and work. It is subsidised by the Ministry of Education, Culture and Science, but also receives money from other parties. CINOP undertakes a number of activities including assisting regional training centres in the development of plans for using ICT; developing and evaluating educational programmes and providing training, information and advice to all providers in the sector.

However, it is possible to rely on competitive pressure to improve quality without resorting to privatisation of provision. In Denmark the taximeter scheme for the finance is designed to increase the quality and efficiency of provision of various forms of initial education, and lifelong learning. First, it puts education institutions under competitive pressure to improve quality. Because education consumers have discretion in choosing their providers (thanks to "school choice" in university education, and the freedom of adults to choose among various adult options), and because providers are paid only for the students they enrol, institutions need to attract students by demonstrating the "quality" of what they provide. Second, the taximeter schemes put institutions under pressure to find more efficient methods for providing their various education and training activities. At the very least, they need to ensure that their costs do not exceed the taximeter rate; to the extent they do, costs need to be subsidised by other activities. To the extent that the taximeter rate exceeds actual costs, the providers can profit from an "efficiency bonus" that provides extra resources that can be used to improve programmes further, or to help develop education in other areas. The taximeter scheme is also used as a tool to influence the mix of training schemes, by providing higher payments in subject areas – information technology, for example – where there is a desire to increase places, or reducing payments in areas of oversupply.

The role of providers in improving the quality of learning opportunities

Whatever the role that national government plays in assuring the quality of lifelong learning opportunities across foundation, tertiary and adult education and training, the ultimate responsibility for delivering high quality programmes still obviously rests with the provider. As indicated above, since the trend across OECD countries is to increase institutional autonomy, this role has consequently grown in importance. Alongside funding mechanisms, national qualifications and standards and national and regional inspection regimes, most OECD countries are focusing their attention in this area on providers undertaking self evaluation against annual plans with targets for improvement. Two examples of how this is managed in different OECD country settings illustrate this point (Box 2.11).

Equity issues

The OECD report *Lifelong Learning for All* raised the problem of equity in its conclusions and saw it as an area which required further consideration:

> "There is evidence that various forms of education and training yield economic returns that more than offset their initial costs. The evidence is most comprehensive in its coverage of formal education and training, although some covers non-formal enterprise-based training as well. The evidence is thinnest with respect to the rates of return on education and training for persons who are

> Box 2.11. **Self-evaluation systems**
>
> In Finland, polytechnics work on a model of management by objectives. There is a three-year agreement between each polytechnic and the Ministry of Education on the target outcomes and measures for improvement for that institution in that year, based on an analysis of results from the previous year. Part of the polytechnics' funding is then based on performance.
>
> In Austria, the act related to *Fachhochschule* institutions requires these institutions to produce an evaluation report every five years which has to be presented and approved by the Council for *Fachhochschulen*. This is a pre-requisite for each *Fachhochschule* to continue to offer courses of study at this level. In addition, a number of new measures for self evaluation of teaching and research have been introduced into Austrian universities. For universities a decree on evaluation also came into force to assess the effectiveness and efficiency of teaching and research. In some universities, courses are assessed by students.

most 'at risk' and who are targets for high priority attention. However, these are precisely the persons for whom the social benefits of lifelong learning may be substantial and, conversely, for whom the social costs of not participating in lifelong learning may be steepest (OECD, 1996, p. 245)."

As this report points out, in order to meet the objective of lifelong learning for all, it is not just a question of increasing participation in lifelong learning, but also ensuring that all have the opportunity to access educational opportunities throughout life, to achieve and to progress within the system. In addition, there is a need to ensure that all groups of learners have their achievements recognised and rewarded in terms of improved employment opportunities and life chances.

According to the OECD report, four groups are particularly disadvantaged as a result of public under-investment in post-school education and training:

- unemployed;
- adults with poor initial education;
- older workers and senior citizens;
- women (in many countries).

OECD countries are well aware of this problem and highlight it in their reports. They also recognise that there is a potential tension between the kind of efficiency measures which they are putting into place and the need to address the issue of equity. There is a strong emphasis in many of the reports on the important role for national government in monitoring the effects of efficiency measures on equality of

© OECD 2000

opportunity and in ensuring that mechanisms are put in place to support those with the greatest need for education and training.

In their discussion of tertiary and adult education provision, all the country reports look at policies for addressing the needs of traditionally disadvantaged groups. There is a particular focus on active labour market initiatives, which are designed to give the unemployed, those in danger of unemployment and those with poor initial education access to both education and training opportunities and experience of work. In many cases, social security and benefits systems are being designed to ensure that there is a greater incentive to undertake education and training or experience of work than to rely on state benefits. There is also an increasing move towards targeted support for fees, grants and loans for those who most need them, rather than the provision of across-the-board entitlements for access to educational opportunities.

This trend is particularly evident in relation to higher education. Many OECD countries have realised that it will not be possible for the public purse to continue to provide free tuition or financial support for all students in higher education, because of the desired and planned increases in participation in this sector. They are, therefore, now considering charging fees for higher education courses, introducing loans rather than grants and reducing the blanket entitlement to maintenance costs, which have traditionally been a feature of many countries' higher education systems. These reforms not only indicate a desire to reduce costs, but also, when combined with targeted support for those students with the greatest financial and social need, allow countries to demonstrate their commitment to widening as well as increasing participation in higher education. Since higher education has traditionally provided the best rates of return to individuals, this kind of policy approach can be seen as addressing issues of equity, as well as increasing the cost-effectiveness of higher education.

Apart from the above measures, which are designed to help those who without financial support would not be able to participate in lifelong learning, some OECD countries are also considering policies which actively advantage those who have traditionally benefited least from their current education and training systems. Hungary, the Netherlands and Sweden are particularly strong in the area of positive discrimination for certain groups of learners to ensure that they genuinely have equality of access to lifelong learning opportunities. In Sweden, for example, the government has continued to fund local universities which are smaller in size and not as cost-effective as their larger counterparts because these local institutions have done a great deal to attract students who would not have previously participated in higher education.

In order to meet their objectives for lifelong learning, OECD countries will need to consider and indeed already are considering policies which not only make their education and training systems more efficient and cost-effective, but which also address issues of equity.

Conclusions

Measures for improving efficiency and cost effectiveness in the lifelong learning process, and improving the quality of outcomes and the benefits of lifelong learning vary from country to country and are related to specific national contexts and priorities. The most obvious involve rationalisation and reorganisation of education and training provision. Often it also involves initiatives to improve recognition of skills and competences, regardless of where they are acquired, so as to allow more "seamless" learning. Measures at the level of the provider to cut the costs of delivery of education and training include reducing the range of courses or programmes on offer in certain institutions or localities; rethinking modes of delivery to provide more flexible entry and exit points for learners; encouraging collaboration between different providers to cut programme development costs and to make more effective use of accommodation and equipment; and, considering the use of information and communications technology (ICT). To enhance the quality of learning outcomes and the benefits that arise from it, governments are devolving decision making authority closer to the point of delivery, while relying more on quality standards for evaluating outcomes.

Many of the measures are at the proposal stage or have only been in place for a limited period of time in most OECD countries. It is difficult to assess, therefore, what difference they have made or are likely to make in terms of either improving the efficiency of lifelong or increasing the benefits and rates of return from lifelong learning. However, in many cases, the OECD countries contributing to this report are laying considerable store by such measures and believe that they will strengthen the incentives for different actors to invest in lifelong learning. Whether this will ultimately make their goals and objectives for lifelong learning more affordable is still, however, in question.

Most country reports recognise that the efficiency measures they are already taking, or are proposing to take, in relation to their education and training systems are likely to make only marginal differences to the affordability of lifelong learning. There is, therefore, considerable consensus within the reports that the major emphasis in the future will need to be on mobilising additional private resources to supplement public funding in this area.

© OECD 2000

Chapter 3

Mobilising Financial Resources for Lifelong Learning

Introduction

Even the strongest incentives to invest in lifelong learning mean nothing unless financial resources are available. There are two factors that have the potential to seriously constrain the availability of financial resources for lifelong learning. One is the fiscal constraints on public spending. It would appear from the discussion that governments cannot pay the costs of all the increased learning activity required. However, to the extent that some increase in spending is possible, there is a question as to whether existing financing mechanisms address the efficiency and equity issues that arise as societies attempt to ensure the affordability of lifelong learning. For example, do they encourage greater cost-effectiveness in the provision of learning opportunities, or do they accommodate shifts in the balance between social and private returns that may occur as learning is spread more over the lifetime of individuals? A second, more particular constraint is on the capacity of the private sector – namely, employers and individuals – to pay for learning. This results from inadequate institutional arrangements (in the form of bank loans at rates of interest comparable to that paid for investment in fixed assets, or taxation policies that allow individuals to pay for training out of pre-tax earnings, for example) that would allow employers and/or individuals to pay the costs of lifelong learning that generates benefits in the future out of past or future earnings. Though "capital markets" for education exist in some countries, in the form of loan programmes for higher education, for example, are they sufficient to meet the financing requirements for all forms of lifelong learning?

This chapter examines how lifelong learning in the different sectors presently is financed and how further investment can be facilitated. The chapter analyses the different mechanisms for providing various actors (providers, learners, employers, individuals and society) with the financial resources to pay for such an investment. It sketches out the principal forms of funding in each sector and sub-sector (foundation learning – including upper secondary schools and apprenticeships; tertiary education; and adult learning), in terms of the distributions of costs and decision-making

© OECD 2000

powers and the effects of each form of funding on efficiency, equity, quality and overall capacity for mobilising resources for expansion.

As the chapter will show, a number of funding policy issues are common across the different sectors :

- Measures commonly have involved two strategies. On the one hand, there is a devolution of financial responsibilities to lower levels, where proximity of financial decision-making to operational realities may encourage greater efficiency. On the other hand, new systems of institutional funding have been introduced in which funding is dependent increasingly on outcomes criteria. Financial devolution, particularly where accompanied by measures to encourage competition between institutions, may encourage greater cost-efficiency in some areas, but may also involve increased transaction costs, due to the local duplication of administrative procedures, the need for extra institutional expenditures on functions like marketing, and need for new forms monitoring. Output-related funding systems provide incentives for improving provider quality and performance but may also entail distortionary pressures on institutions (to "cream" or "skim" good students, and misrepresent outcomes) which, if not carefully monitored, can also negatively effects equity and standards. Close monitoring of performance also incurs extra costs.

- Authorities also are seeking ways to increase private investments in education and training to meet the increasing costs of lifelong learning, though policies and mechanisms in this area are not nearly so developed. Policy measures that have been initiated are discussed below. The main issues which arise here are how to devise schemes which distribute costs of education and training equitably between the different beneficiaries, without reducing access and equality of opportunity to individuals with unequal private resources, and without engendering levels of regulation on companies which reduce flexibility, enterprise and innovation.

In addressing these issues, authorities seek to devise financing mechanisms that not only provide financial resources, but which do so in such a way as to provide incentives to increase efficiency in provision of lifelong learning, and raise the quality of outputs.

The country reports provide ample evidence of policy innovation. However, there is little evidence as to the effects of different schemes with respect to generating net new financial resources, or interactions with cost-effectiveness and/or quality. Many are in the early phases of implementation and there are very few reports of reliable evaluation studies on the effects of different policies.

The discussion below examines financing arrangements and issues across three broad "sectors" of lifelong learning: secondary education and vocational training; tertiary education; and adult learning.

Secondary education and initial training: principal issues

The upper secondary level represents a distinct sector in all countries, although it may sometimes comprise institutions that lead directly to other levels of education and training. Generally speaking it involves students learning after the age of compulsory full-time schooling and who are taking courses preparing them for direct entry to skilled work or further study in the tertiary or higher education sectors. Apprentices, although employed on special apprentice or training contracts, are also generally included in the category of those undergoing upper secondary level learning. The typical ages of students in this sector vary by country, according to the age at which they start (normally 15 or 16 in the sample countries) and according to how long students are permitted to continue studying at this level. The majority of students at this level in all countries, however, are past the compulsory school leaving age (for full-time students) and below 21 years. The sector includes a variety of institutions which are specific to it, such as general high schools, vocational high schools and apprentice schools, as well as the upper stages of institutions which also serve other sectors (*e.g.* the senior sections of the Austrian Higher Academic and Technical Schools and Colleges). The relative institutional specificity of the sector, and the specific objectives which are assigned to it, have generally led to specific policies regarding resourcing and its objectives, and to specific funding mechanisms. It is therefore possible to treat this sector as distinctive with regards to funding issues, although issues and systems will inevitably overlap with other sectors and other categories of students.

The principal policy issues in the funding of this sector have been:

– How to achieve maximum participation and higher levels of achievement within the sector.

– How to reduce barriers to access for under-represented groups into different branches within the sector and thus to enhance equity.

– How to increase cost-effectiveness in provision to help make the system affordable.

– How to increase the level and transparency of benefits from investment in the sector to encourage and justify further investment.

– How to provide incentives to encourage new forms of investment in learning at this level.

Various policies have been adopted in the different countries to increase incentives to investment by improving quality of outcomes and cost-effectiveness. These

© OECD 2000

include a wide variety of funding and incentive mechanisms for both providers and learners. These are considered below in relation to mechanisms for the funding of upper secondary schools (general and vocational), the funding of apprentice schools and direct support of learners.

Upper secondary schools

All countries have a mix of types of upper secondary schools where some are designated private and some public. The ratio between the two varies considerably between countries where schools designated as private or "independent" enrol large a number of students (such as the Netherlands, Japan and South Korea) and countries where they are relatively insignificant in numerical terms (*e.g.* Sweden). In all countries, the majority of funding for upper secondary schools comes from the public sector, although the level of private investment in upper secondary education varies significantly. Private investments are made primarily by students, parents of students, sponsors and donors and by employers through the financing of enterprise-based employment training and taxes levied for this and other forms of provision in the sector. Their total contribution to spending in the sector varies depending on such factors as whether the public schools charge fees (as in Japan and South Korea), the relative proportion of private schools and the level of state subsidy they receive, the degree of employer investment in training and the degree of state support for students. The overall balance between public and private investments, and the efficiency and equity of particular institutional arrangements influence the extent to which societies can afford to expand opportunities for lifelong learning at this level and increase their accessibility. Different funding systems have been adopted in different countries with a variety of effects relative to these issues.

Tables 3.1*a* through 3.1*d* examine these different approaches with regard to their implications for efficiency, equity, and other criteria, such as the incentive to increase participation or stimulate new resources. In doing so, the tables distinguish between the roles played by different levels of government. In terms of funding flows, this involves differences in the relative proportions of funds which originate at central, regional and local levels of public authority, and in differences in the paths that these funds follow. Central governments may pay all the costs of upper secondary schools directly to provider institutions or they may channel the funds through regional or local authorities. Alternatively, funds to schools may be distributed by regional or local authorities, where some or all of these funds are rebated to the authorities by central government. These different systems of public funding flows have different effects. Direct or indirect funding by central government may be used to ensure equality of resources available in each local area, whereas funding from regional and local taxes may result in regional inequalities in resourcing, unless accompanied by regionally redistributive central funding. On the other hand, maximising the role of the regional and local authorities in allocating funding to institutions, involves decentralising decision-making which may improve efficiency and local responsiveness.

Funding systems also may differ with respect to the way in which funds are distributed to institutional providers and how these may be used by providers. The main question here is not what level of government distributes the funds (central, regional or local authority), but rather what criteria are used for their distribution and how much discretion the provider has over their use. Analysis here can be difficult, because not all countries use a consistent national formula even for a given type of school. In some countries, where funds are distributed at the regional or local level, the distributing authorities are allowed within limits to determine their own criteria for allocations to institutions (as in South Korea and the Czech Republic) which leads to a diversity of funding systems.

Despite these difficulties, however, one can distinguish between the principal types of funding systems which have significantly different effects. The main differences here are between systems based primarily on inputs and those based on a mixture of inputs and outputs, and between those which give the recipient institutions discretion over the use of funds and those which do not:

- In "input-based" systems institutional funding levels are determined principally according to the projected real costs of the major components *i.e.* staffing and non-staff expenditures, usually calculated as a function of past or planned student enrolments on different types of programmes and the average costs of staffing and building capacity allowed for each type of course enrollee.

- In the "input-outcome" based systems, funding is awarded partly on the basis of input, and partly on the basis of whether certain outcomes or performance is achieved. The inclusion of the outcome factor is intended to provide an incentive for improving quality and effectiveness of provision, although it may, at the same time, lead to certain distortions in patterns of delivery, such as "skimming" or "creaming": biasing enrolments towards individuals who already are closest to the programme objective (and therefore most likely to successfully complete), rather than those likely to gain the most.

- Either model can be associated with "delegated budgetary powers" which allow institutions to reallocate spending across different budget headings. Increased financial delegation is sometimes promoted in order to increase institutional efficiency.

© OECD 2000

Table 3.1a **Upper secondary education financing schemes: central government pays**

Different types of schemes	Efficiency			Equity	Other criteria		
	Increasing benefits	Decreasing costs	Other impacts on cost-effectiveness		Generating new resources	Increasing participation	Generating new finance partnerships
Austrian Allgemeinbildende und Berufsbildende Höhere Schulen: Federal government directly finances full costs to schools on input costs basis.	Weak funding incentives to quality.	Weak incentives to cost reduction.	No incentives for distortions such as "skimming".	High access and equity between regions.	No effect.	Good access for those qualified.	New financial partnerships possible.
Danish Taximeter scheme: Central government sets payment schedule according to historical cost; payment is contingent on successful outcomes.	Encourages institutions to compete for students on basis of quality.	Strong incentive to reduce costs to approved rate and further.	Periodic review of rates maintains pressure on ensuring cost-effectiveness.	n.a.	Creates open-ended obligation for state to meet demand.	Encourages learner choice.	Generating finance partnerships.

n.a. not applicable.
Source: Country reports.

Mobilising Financial Resources for Lifelong Learning

Table 3.1b. **Upper secondary education financing schemes: mixed-level state funding**

Different types of schemes	Efficiency			Equity	Other criteria		
	Increasing benefits	Decreasing costs	Other impacts on cost-effectiveness		Generating new resources	Increasing participation	Generating new finance partnerships
Austrian polytechnical schools: Local authorities fund capital and non-teaching staff costs; regional authorities fund teaching staff with refund from *Bund*.	Incentives for quality in normative criteria.	n.a.	No incentives for distortions such as "skimming" (selecting only the most advantaged students).	No regional inequalities in teacher staffing but some in other areas.	Some effect from new opportunities financial partnerships.	Open access increases participation.	Regional and local government partnerships.
Austrian apprenticeship system	n.a.	No effects.	n.a.	Wide access.	Employer funding.	High participation.	Regional and local government partnerships.
Czech upper secondary schools: Central government provides vast majority of funds with local government contributing a little. Central funding according to weighted student numbers – institutional funds by normative criteria.	Incentives for improving outcomes.	Adjusting unit funding on normatives may incentivise lower costs.	May create incentives for distortions such as "skimming".	Normatives may have distorting effects on access.	Encourages income generation.	Encourages participation.	Links with private sector clients.
Swedish upper secondary schools: Schools funded from municipalities on per capita basis from local taxes and central government grants.	Monopoly regional providers: weak incentives to quality.	Weak incentives to efficiency.	Incentive to maximise students on roll.	Comprehensive schools have high equity in access but regional inequalities due to different local tax bases.	No effect.	Access creates high participation.	No effect.

© OECD 2000

Table 3.1b. **Upper secondary education financing schemes: mixed-level state funding** (cont.)

| Different types of schemes | Criteria for evaluating financing schemes |||||||
| | Efficiency || Equity | Generating new resources | Other criteria ||
	Increasing benefits	Decreasing costs	Other impacts on cost-effectiveness			Increasing participation	Generating new finance partnerships
Dutch upper secondary schools: Largely funded by central government on inputs model with some local funding. Fees charges for extras. Institutions receive lump sum budgets and can do contract work. Competition from school choice. Plans for performance-related component. "Free School Tradition".	School choice encourages quality.	Financial devolution encourages cost saving.	n.a.	Access to schools dependent on availability of suitable stream.	Encourages income-generating contract work.	Encourages learner choice.	Encourages new foundations of free schools.
Norwegian upper secondary schools: Financed by the county authorities with support from the central government. The county authorities enjoy greater autonomy in the provision of education.	Increased benefits by improved co-ordination of the public measures, more flexible organisation of education and training, and better system for documentation of non-formal learning.	No effect.	No effect.	High equality in access for 16-19 year-olds, but might have regional inequalities. Adults have no statutory right to education – participation since 1994 has been decreasing.	No effect.	n.a.	n.a.

Table 3.1b. **Upper secondary education financing schemes: mixed-level state funding** (*cont.*)

Different types of schemes	Criteria for evaluating financing schemes					
	Efficiency			Equity	Other criteria	
	Increasing benefits	Decreasing costs	Other impacts on cost-effectiveness		Generating new resources	Increasing participation	Generating new finance partnerships
Norwegian apprentice training: Government grants are given to enterprises which take on apprentices – additional funds for disabled.	Incentive for quality – enterprises receive additional grants when apprenticeship period is successfully completed.	Substantial effect: school-based training more expensive.	No effect.	Mismatch problem in supply and demand of apprenticeship places.	No effect.	n.a.	n.a.

n.a. not applicable.
Source: Country reports.

Table 3.1c. **Upper secondary education financing schemes: mixed state and private funding**

Different types of schemes	Criteria for evaluating financing schemes							
	Increasing benefits	Efficiency		Equity	Other criteria		
		Decreasing costs	Other impacts on cost-effectiveness		Generating new resources	Increasing participation	Generating new finance partnerships
Japanese municipal and prefectural upper secondary schools: Funding sourced from prefectural and municipal taxes and loans, fees, and central government grant designed to equalise regional funds. Institutions funded on inputs.	Incentives to quality from ranking of schools.	High staff student ratios funding standards reduce costs. Fees contributions reduce public costs.	High space utilisation.	Equity reduced by ranking of institutions and competition with private schools which not all can afford. Reasonable equity of provision between regions.	Fees and loans generate additional resources.	Per capita funding incentivises high recruitment. Establishment of new types of school to meet student demands.	No effect.
Korean public upper secondary schools: Funded in part from fees and local taxes but mainly from central government. Institutional funding mainly by student and classroom numbers.	Incentives to quality from ranking of schools.	High staff student ratios funding standards reduce costs. Fees contributions reduce public costs.	High space utilisation	Some inequalities between regions.	Fees generate additional resources. Firms may co-fund.	High recruitment encouraged by per capita funding.	Vocational high schools can have collaborative links with firms.

Source: Country reports.

Mobilising Financial Resources for Lifelong Learning

Table 3.1d. **Upper secondary education financing schemes: state-subsidised private schools**

Different types of schemes	Criteria for evaluating financing schemes							
	Efficiency				Equity	Other criteria		
	Increasing benefits	Decreasing costs	Other impacts on cost-effectiveness			Generating new resources	Increasing participation	Generating new finance partnerships
Austrian private upper secondary schools: Charge fees but church schools receive central government funds to cover all teacher costs.	Market incentive to quality.	Incentives to reduce costs against fixed fee element of funding in non-state-funded schools.	Reimbursement of teacher costs in church schools discourages cost reduction on teaching.		Access dependent on ability to pay and selection which reduces equity.	Generates fee income.	Provides greater choice.	No effect.
Japanese private high schools: Funded from fees (45%), central and prefectural government, donations and property interest. Regulated.	Market incentive to quality in competitive recruitment system.	Strong incentive to reduce costs against fee element.	Incentive for efficient space utilisation from property owner-ship. Incentives for large classes.		Access dependent on supply of schools, ability to pay and selection.	Generates fee income.	Provides greater choice in high participation system.	Promotes founding of new schools and private sponsorship.
Korean private high schools: Funding from fees, central government grant, property income and donation.	Market incentive to quality in competitive recruitment system.	Strong incentive to reduce costs against fee element.	Incentive for efficient space utilisation from property owner-ship.		Negative effects on equity reduced by government maintaining fee levels at parity with public schools. Scholarships for fees also available.	Generates fee income.	Provides greater choice in high participation system.	Tax breaks promote founding of new schools and private sponsorship.
Czech private secular schools: Set own fees and receive state subsidy for recurrent costs according to normatives.	Market incentive to quality. Output criteria being designed to try to promote quality.	Adjustment of unit funding may promote cost reduction.	Low regulation may detract from quality. Distortionary effects.		Unregulated fees undermine equity in access and quality.	Generates fee income.	Provides greater choice although quality may be uneven.	Encourages new foundations.

Source: Country reports.

Funding models: public upper secondary schools

Three main models may be distinguished from the country reports:

1) Direct funding from central government (on input model – no fees)

In this model, central government provides for all capital and recurrent costs of schools and funds them directly according to an input model of costs. An example of this would be the funding of the *Allgemeinbildende und Berufsbildende Höhere Schulen* (academic and technical secondary schools) in Austria.

2) Mixed-level state funding (no fees)

This model also involves full public funding but sourced at different levels of the state, and distributed from lower levels. Central government grants to lower levels are normally calculated according to needs (in terms of potential students and measures of need), but locally provided revenues may vary according to local priorities and local tax revenues, leading to possible regional variation in funding to institutions. The country case studies provide the following examples:

- In Sweden, upper secondary schools are funded partly from local taxes and partly from central government grants to municipalities. Local resources are not equalised. Models for institutional allocations vary by region, but are usually on a *per capita* basis. The municipality funds its own institutions and also the costs of students studying in institutions in other localities in certain cases.
- The Austrian polytechnical schools (prevocational school) is funded by the local authorities for capital investment and non-teaching staff costs and by the regional authorities for teaching costs, with the latter fully refundable from the *Bund*.
- In the Czech Republic, public upper secondary schools are funded by central government and local authorities, but with central government funding over 95%. Central government funds the district offices according to a formula based on student numbers, types of school and types of course. The district offices allocate funds to institutions according to different models but generally these are based on complex formulae involving numerous "normatives", some of which relate to performance measures.
- In Norway, upper secondary schools are funded from central government grants to the county municipalities. The education authorities in the counties administer both the upper secondary schools and the apprenticeship measures. The public upper secondary schools are free of charge for both young people and adults. School books and other materials are in principal paid for by the individual, but loans and grants from the State Educational Loan fund

© OECD 2000

cover reasonable subsistence costs. Grants are also calculated taking into account the cost of learning materials.

3) Mixed-state funding with private subsidy

This model is distinctive in two ways. Central government funding to lower levels is designed to equalise resources across regions and fees are charged at public upper secondary schools. Two examples of this type of funding are given:

- In Japan, upper secondary schools charge fees (equivalent to about 10% of costs) and the remainder of funding comes from the municipal or prefectural authority responsible for the school. These authorities derive their funds from local taxes, long-term loans, and from the central government grants which are designed to compensate for the variations in local revenues and subsidise capital outlay. Institutions are funded according to a formula based on student and staff numbers (according to standardised ratios and costs) with some ear-marked funding for special purposes.
- In Korea, public upper secondary school revenues derive partly from fees and predominantly from allocations from provincial offices which are calculated according to different models in different areas, but which are usually determined by numbers of students and classrooms. Local government taxes provide a small part of the revenues which the provincial offices can spend, but the majority comes from central government according to a model which seeks to equalise local resources.

Funding models: private upper secondary schools

There are three main models of private high school funding in the case study countries:

1) Fees with state subsidy and regulation

The most common model is for private schools to charge fees and to be additionally eligible for state subsidies subject to their meeting certain criteria and being submitted to national regulation.

In Austria, private schools can charge fees and some of these, including all church schools, receive subsidies from the *Bund* to cover staff costs.

In Japan and South Korea, private funding plays a large part in paying for private upper secondary education. Japanese high schools derive their revenues from fees (45%), national government (29.8%), loans (9.8%), properties income (6.9%) and donations (2%). South Korean high schools rely on similar sources although the exact distributions are not known. Fees are set at parity with public high schools to maintain equity.

© OECD 2000

2) Fees with state subsidy but without regulation

Private schools in the Czech Republic can set their own fees and are only partly regulated by the state. Private schools are also subsidised by the central government for recurrent costs according to the "normatives", as with the funding of public schools. Normatives for private schools are reduced to some extent and their real size depends on some (rather formal) conditions which they have to fulfil.

3) Government funded without fees

According to the law in the Netherlands schools can be set up by private bodies and individuals providing they can demonstrate sufficient public support and providing they meet the stiff criteria for the operating of all national schools. These "private" schools are autonomous foundations, but they cannot charge fees (except for "extras") and they are fully funded from public, mostly central government, sources. Central government funds personnel on the basis of average costs for staff whose numbers are determined according to a fixed ratio between different types of staff and students, and according to the numbers in the previous year. Materials and equipment costs are funded by central government according to student numbers and floor space weighted for different types of school. Allocations to schools are made in lump sums and allow schools to reallocate across budget headings. Schools can also receive funds for contracts in the private sector. There are currently plans to introduce a performance-related element into the funding.

Apprenticeships

Apprenticeships which involve both enterprise-based and school-based education and training are normally funded from a combination of public and private funds. Typically, as in Austria, employers will fund the training which occurs on site (including the costs of instruction, damage and foregone production) whilst the state funds the costs of the *Berufsschulen* (fifty-fifty central and *Länder* governments). Students contribute through their productivity and through earnings foregone (trainee wages being lower). The Czech apprentice system has also worked on this model, although recently the state has been forced to take on the costs of on-site training where the employers cannot carry this.

The Norwegian apprenticeship model consists of two years at school plus two years of apprenticeship. During the two years with the enterprise the apprentice will have one year of training and take part in productive work for one year. Education is free for apprentices, who in addition receive a wage for their work participation in the enterprise. The apprentice is engaged by the enterprise from the first day and is paid the equivalent of one year's salary over two years. The salary is stipulated in the wage agreement of the trade and is about half the amount of what skilled workers receive. Enterprises that provide training for apprentices receive government grants.

Support for learners in secondary education and initial training

Students in upper secondary education bear various costs including those of fees, accommodation, subsistence, textbooks, materials and study school trips. In addition to parental financial support and the students' own contributions from part-time earnings, there are various other sources of public support in each of the case study countries. These include:

1) Family allowances (income-related and non-income-related)

These are paid to parents of students. The Netherlands offer non-means-tested family allowances for the under 18s. In Austria family allowances are means-tested.

2) Study grants (income-related and non-income related)

Sweden and Norway have both kinds of study grant available to different types of student. Austria has means-tested grants for able but impoverished students. Pupils above 18 in upper secondary vocational education in the Netherlands also receive grants.

3) Accommodation allowances

Austria provides means-tested accommodation allowances for upper secondary students who have to board. Finland also provides allowances for accommodation and meals in certain cases.

4) Textbook and special costs grants

All students in Austria receive textbooks but pay a small contribution. Hungary provides funds for textbooks for certain categories of student.

5) Travel grants

Provided by Austria, Finland, Norway and several other countries in certain cases. In the case of Austria, parents or students pay a small contribution to travel grants.

6) Scholarships

These are for needy and able students and are provided by local authorities in Japan.

© OECD 2000

7) Loans (interest-free or interest-bearing)

This system of support is in operation in Finland, Japan, Norway and elsewhere. In Finland private banks are used with loans at market rates with the state acting as guarantor.

The rationale for financing arrangements in secondary education and training

Governments are the principal sources of finance of foundation learning in all case study countries. They meet the majority of the capital and recurrent costs in schools and, in some countries, provide substantial subsidies toward student maintenance. Individual students and their families pay a much lower share of costs directly in all countries, although the proportion varies significantly. In most countries where the majority of upper secondary schools are free at the point of access, individual contributions are limited mainly to maintenance and incidental study expenses. In countries where fees are charged in the majority of schools (*e.g.* Japan and South Korea) direct individual contributions are substantially higher. Direct employer contributions to foundation learning are also limited in most countries. The most substantial contributions are made in countries with extensive apprenticeship systems, where employers pay the costs associated with enterprise-based training components, or in countries which impose training levies on firms above a certain size (*e.g.* the *taxe d'apprentissage* in France) which are used towards paying the costs of foundation learning.

The principal of state funding of foundation learning is generally based on three premises. Firstly, the social returns to schooling at this level – in terms of enhanced national productivity and collective social benefits – are normally thought to be high thus justifying the socialisation of costs. Secondly, upper secondary learning has become virtually indispensable for gaining qualified work in most countries, thus making the sector *de facto* a part of the compulsory education system and access to it a virtual right for young people. Thirdly, since learning at this level is a virtual necessity and right, equity demands a high level of public financing to ensure a reasonable equality of access regardless of ability to pay. These principals are upheld to a greater or lesser extent in all countries. However, other considerations bear on the issue which lead to significant national variations in the shares of costs falling to other actors.

Individuals and enterprises both receive substantial private returns from foundation learning. Individuals who qualify at upper secondary level have access to qualified jobs and further education and training not available to those who leave school at the end of lower secondary education, and they may therefore expect to earn substantially more than the latter over time. Firms benefit from having access to a ready supply of young people with sufficient foundations in learning for them to be easily and inexpensively trained and who, in some cases, already possess occupational skills which may be put to productive use. Neither the individual nor the company can capture all the returns to any investments made to learning at this level, and nor can they be certain of what returns will accrue specifically to themselves. However, they clearly do derive some future benefit. In some countries this is recognised in the contributions which different parties are expected to make – in Japan and South Korea, for instance, through substantial individual contributions to fees; and, in countries like Austria, Italy and France, through employer contributions to the cost of apprenticeship training.

There are both advantages and disadvantages to systems which rely significantly on individual and employer contributions to foundation learning, although the disadvantages lie mainly with the requirement for individual contributions. Employer contributions can generally be justified in that the employers receive substantial benefits. Provided that employers can be incentivised, through regulation or persuasion, to invest in apprentice learning there is a considerable overall advantage in that this generates additional resources and targets these resources towards training that is relevant to employer needs. The disadvantages, inherent in the apprenticeship system itself as a means of training, are that foundation skills training can become overly specialised and geared towards meeting short-term employer needs, rather than promoting labour market flexibility and long-term skills development for the individual and national economy. In countries which have the institutional foundations for an extensive apprenticeship system, this trade-off has generally been considered acceptable, especially given that measures can and are being taken to use regulations to broaden the basis of apprentice training.

Substantial individual contributions to meeting the costs of upper secondary provision are justified on the grounds that individuals also benefit and these contributions have the advantage that they lead to substantial additional investment. In the cases of Japan, indeed, it is clear that individual contributions to upper secondary schooling through the payment of fees has been a major enabling factor behind the massive expansion of the system since the 1960s. In particular, complementary public and private financing of private schools has been used to achieve a massive leverage of additional investment. However, this has come at a cost in terms of government capacity to regulate the upper secondary system and, increasingly, in terms of equity. The explosion of private investment in high school education has been associated with excessive credentialism and over-heated examination competition, the effects of which are now widely regarded as dysfunctional; the costs of fees are placing an intolerable financial burden on many families; and the proliferation of private high schools which charge fees beyond the means of some families leads to increasing inequalities in access to upper secondary education, especially as private schools are now tending to move towards the top of the school hierarchy.

For most countries, with already extensive systems of upper secondary schools, increased contributions from individuals through fees for schools would be too

© OECD 2000

damaging to equity to be acceptable as a means of generating additional resources, especially since education at this level is now becoming more or less synonymous with compulsory education. Increased contribution from employers through investment in apprenticeship training is generally believed to be desirable, but is not easy to achieve. Successful and extensive apprentice systems require specific institutional foundations, forms of social partnership and levels of government regulation which are not readily achievable or acceptable in all countries, and which may even be hard to sustain in countries which have exhibited them to date.

In terms of the funding of learners, there are similar arguments in favour of the sharing of costs according to benefits and similar trade-offs between incentivising investment and maintaining equity. Countries which provide little state support for learners encourage individual investment and thus generate increasing resources for learners. However, they also risk creating barriers to participation among young people from families who are unable to pay, or obstacles to achievement amongst young people forced to earn their way through their studies. On the other hand countries like Sweden and Norway, which provide generous state financial support to learners, maintain high levels of equity but place heavy demands on public resources which must also be used to finance provision. Forms of state support which are targeted at specific groups in dangers of exclusion from participation are most likely to enhance equity without unacceptable public cost. They have the disadvantage of leaving students from families with levels of income which disqualify them from state support dependent on their families, but this may be a diminishing consideration as the Dutch report illustrates, since enhanced supply makes studying locally the norm.

Effects on equity and efficiency in secondary education and training

Equity considerations figure large in debates about the funding of the upper secondary sector, as the above discussion illustrates. In principal, those who benefit from foundation learning should make corresponding contributions to its costs, except where unacceptable inequities result. In the debate about distributing the costs of learning these inequities mainly relate to effects on individual access. Although all individuals may expect to benefit in the long-term from upper secondary learning, they may not all have the current resources to finance their contributions. Benefits are long-term, but costs are immediate and market imperfections limit the availability of capital to finance individual investment in learning for which returns are long-term and uncertain. Public financing has therefore been necessary to ensure reasonable equity in access to upper secondary education and training. In countries with mature systems of mass upper secondary education, provision is mainly delivered through public schools which charge no fees, or only very low fees.

In addition to these, there are other issues of equity that arise from different systems of funding. Generally speaking, the more centralised a funding system is, the more capacity it has for ensuring equality in funding between different regions and between different institutions. Funding systems which rely in part on contributions from local taxes run the risk of creating inequalities between regions with some contributing more than others to education, either because they have richer tax bases or because they allocate more of their tax revenue to education. Compensation for this factor can be achieved through refunds from central government designed to equalise levels of regional funding, but these are open to the objection that they give regional autonomy with the one hand and take it away with the other.

Institutional funding systems involve similar trade-offs between equity, efficiency and autonomy. Funding systems which allow individual institutions maximum autonomy in the utilisation of resources may encourage greater efficiency, especially when institutions are competing for funds on the basis of student enrolments and achievements. However, they may also tend to encourage increasing inequalities between institutions in terms of the extent and quality of their provision, and their overall resource levels.

Systems based on competitive *per capita* funding of institutions, where institutions are funded according to the number of (full-time equivalent) students they enrol, provide strong cost-efficiency incentives and have the capacity to drive down costs significantly. But they may, at the same time, have negative effects on quality, if other safeguards are not built in. Institutions have an interest in maintaining quality in as much as their reputation and ability to recruit students depends on it. However, given that a competitive market in upper secondary education is often constrained by limited choice in accessible suppliers for students, and also by inadequate information on the relative quality of different suppliers, this may not be sufficient to ensure quality. Allocation systems which include an element of performance-related funding (colleges in England and Wales) alleviate this problem by providing incentives for good quality provision. However, these systems can also lead to various distortions. Institutions may be encouraged to "cream" (to recruit only those students most likely to meet the performance criteria); they may try to enrol students in courses below their potential in order to maximise their chances of meeting the performance criteria; or they may be tempted, where they are responsible for assessing students, to lower their standards to ensure that more achieve the performance criteria. None of these problems are in principal insoluble, providing that adequate measures can be designed and providing that funding systems use them in ways which are smart enough to incentivise both efficiency and quality. There is inadequate evidence to date from countries which have experimented with different institutional funding models to ascertain which of these models would meet these criteria.

© OECD 2000

Tertiary education

The financing of tertiary education has become an increasingly controversial topic in many OECD countries in recent years. Demand for places and actual enrolments have risen dramatically both for short and long duration tertiary education courses and continues to rise. This has placed growing pressure on the budgets of governments which have traditionally met the majority of costs for tertiary education in most countries. It has also forced urgent consideration of new ways of reducing costs of provision and financing these costs.

Increased participation in tertiary education is generally believed to be important for sustaining national economic competitiveness, and governments have, on the whole, felt bound to meet the rising demand for places. However, individuals who participate in tertiary education tend to receive substantial lifetime benefits, not least in the higher incomes which accrue to graduates, and this poses stark questions about how much they should contribute to the costs and when. Up until now there has been little symmetry within public tertiary education between the relative benefits and costs for the various parties concerned. Employers and students have made fairly slight contributions to the costs although receiving substantial benefits. This situation has been allowed on the grounds that requiring greater contributions might deter able young people from entering tertiary education to the detriment of the national pool of skills, and also on grounds of equity. The wage returns to tertiary education are not entirely predictable and they vary for different social groups and depending on what occupation the graduates enter. They also involve a considerable time lag between investment and returns. These risks can act as a deterrent to investment and have acted as a justification for public financing. However, current financial pressures have forced a new look at these issues in many countries.

Financing models

Tertiary education institutions receive their revenues from a variety of different sources, including student fees, funding for private contracting, and government funding of teaching and research (Tables 3.2*a* – 3.2*c*). Different national funding systems can be distinguished according to the relative weight of each of these sources in overall funding. Important distinctions also exist in the ways and the criteria used by governments to calculate the allocations of public funding for teaching and research to the individual institutions. Teaching may be funded largely on the basis of student enrolments, that is in terms of the average actual costs of teaching students on particular types of programme. Alternatively, it may be funded on the basis of a combination of enrolment and performance criteria, where a certain sum is available for each student enrolled and further sums dependent on certain measures of success of student learning. Likewise with research funding, funds may be distributed according to the number of academic staff employed in an institution who are active or supposed to be active in research, or on the basis of the success of the institution on various measures of research performance (*e.g.* research grants obtained, research student graduations, publications). From the country reports considered here, we can broadly distinguish between three types of funding systems which differ according to the relative weight placed on each of these factors. There are, of course, numerous variations on these broad types, and not all countries can be assigned to the types due to lack of data. However, for illustrative purposes, the following distinctions can be made.

Government funding with substantial fee contribution

On this model, student fees constitute a substantial proportion of the funds for tertiary education. In private institutions, they may come near to representing full real costs, with only a small government subsidy. In public institutions, their share of costs would be lower, but still substantial. Institutions may receive some income from private contract work in research or consultancy, and the remainder of costs are born by government, usually in the form of grants calculated on the basis of standardised input costs based on student and staff number ratios.

In Japan, the majority of students go to private universities (76%). These derive their revenues predominantly from fees (50%), with a small government contribution (8.1%) and a rising contract fee element from enterprises (about 33%). Public universities are divided between the national universities, which are funded directly from central government, and the prefectural and municipal universities which are funded by the regional authorities which receive their funds from central government. Revenues for public universities derive in part from fees (about 12%) and in part from endowments, donations, property interest and loans. Central government, however, is the source for the large majority of funding. Central government funding is calculated primarily on the basis of student numbers and is standardised against the input costs associated with them.

Korea also has a majority of private universities which derive most of their funds from fees and tuition (73%). Public institutions also charge fees and receive some funds from contract work, but a substantial part of their funding comes direct from central government.

Government funding without substantial fee contribution

In this model, higher education institutions charge no fees and receive only a small part of their income from private donations and contract work. The vast majority of funding comes directly from central government.

In Sweden, higher education institutions charge no fees and receive almost all their funding direct from government. Since 1993, government grants have been allocated according to a mixture of input and performance criteria. Funds to institutions

© OECD 2000

Table 3.2a. **Higher education financing schemes: government funding with substantial fee contribution**

Different types of schemes	Criteria for evaluating financing schemes						
	Efficiency				Other criteria		
	Increasing benefits	Decreasing costs	Other impacts on cost-effectiveness	Equity	Generating new resources	Increasing participation	Generating new finance partnerships
Japan: Majority private universities funded largely from fees with small government subsidy; public universities charge lower fees and mostly funded by central or municipal government. Some contract work. Institutional funding on inputs.	Private universities have market incentives for quality. Public universities incentivised to maximise reputation. However, students earning during studies may reduce performance.	Private universities incentivised to reduce costs against fees. Public universities have only weak incentive to reduce costs.	No strong financial incentives to improve research performance from government funding scheme, but incentive from market for contract work in private universities.	Low on equity. Access to universities dependent on supply, student ability to pass entrance exams, and on ability to pay. Scholarship schemes for most able mitigate negative effect of fees on equity.	Private universities generate new resources through fees and donations.	Diversity of providers promote high participation.	Only weak links with other partners. Government currently trying to encourage various sources of revenue.
Danish Taximeter scheme	Encourages institution to compete for students on basis of quality.	Strong incentive to reduce costs to approved rate and further.	Periodic review of rates maintains pressures on ensuring cost-effectiveness.		Creates open-ended obligation for state to meet demand.	Encourages learner choice.	Generating finance partnerships.

Source: Country reports.

Mobilising Financial Resources for Lifelong Learning

Table 3.2a. **Higher education financing schemes: government funding with substantial fee contribution** (*cont.*)

Different types of schemes	Criteria for evaluating financing schemes							
	Efficiency			Equity	Generating new resources	Other criteria	
	Increasing benefits	Decreasing costs	Other impacts on cost-effectiveness			Increasing participation	Generating new finance partnerships
Korea: Majority private universities funded largely from fees with small government subsidy; public universities charge lower fees and mostly funded by central or municipal government. Some contract work. Institutional funding on inputs.	Private universities have market incentives for quality. Public universities incentivised to quality to maximise reputation. However, surplus of demand to supply reduces market impact on quality. However, students earning during studies may reduce performance.	Private universities incentivised to reduce costs against fees. Public universities have only weak incentive to reduce costs.	System promotes homogeneous provision of general courses with bias to cheaper non-science subjects.	Low on equity. Access to universities dependent on supply and on ability to pay. Scholarship schemes mitigate this for most able.	Private universities generate new resources through fees and donations.	Diversity of providers and high returns for graduates promote high participation.	Only weak links with other partners. Government currently trying to encourage university-firm partnerships.

Source: Country reports.

Table 3.2b. **Higher education financing schemes: government funding with no fees**

Different types of schemes	Criteria for evaluating financing schemes						
	Efficiency			Equity	Generating new resources	Other criteria	
	Increasing benefits	Decreasing costs	Other impacts on cost-effectiveness			Increasing participation	Generating new finance partnerships
Norway: Institutions receive majority of funds from central government, with additional income from contract work.	n.a.	Incentives to reduce costs through financial devolution.	Subject weightings help avoid skew towards cheaper courses.	High levels of access due to absence of fees. Large capacity in tertiary education institutions.	Some external financing of teachers: extensive contract research.	High access, high participation.	Some incentives to collaborate.
Sweden: Universities receive majority of funds from central government. Institutional funding in lump sums according to input and performance criteria.	Strong incentives to quality.	Some incentives to reduce costs through financial devolution.	Subject weightings help avoid skew towards cheaper courses.	High levels of access due to absence of fees and selection in most areas.	Low incentives to generate additional income.	High access, high participation.	Few incentives to collaborate.
Austria: Courses at *Fachhochschulen* are funded by the federal government on the basis of weighted student numbers (unit costs). Additional income from local, regional governments, social partners, firms.	Courses are created for a maximum duration of five years. Evaluation (internal report and peer group) is decisive for further accreditation and government subsidy.	Some incentives to reduce costs through financial devolution.	Subject weightings help avoid skew towards cheaper courses.	Selectivity reduces general access but widening of regional provisions and reduced drop-out rates counterbalance inequality in access.	Low incentives to generate additional income. A mixed funding system has been established in the sector of *Fachhochschulen* (federal, regional, local governments, social partners, firms).	Regional disparities in higher education provision have been reduced and thus regional access has been increased.	The system of mixed funding gave rise to new finance partnerships (see first and sixth column).

© OECD 2000

Table 3.2b. **Higher education financing schemes: government funding with no fees** (cont.)

Different types of schemes	Criteria for evaluating financing schemes							
	Efficiency			Equity	Other criteria			
	Increasing benefits	Decreasing costs	Other impacts on cost-effectiveness		Generating new resources	Increasing participation	Generating new finance partnerships	
Austria: Universities funded primarily from central government with inter-university planning. Recent introduction of devolution.	Funding system gives weak incentives to quality.	Some incentives to reduce costs through financial devolution.	n.a.	Open access.	Low incentives to generate additional income.	n.a.	Universities generate additional income through research contracts and continuing education activities.	
Czech Republic: Majority of universities public with most funding from central government. Some contract work. Faculties funded by "normatives".	Some incentives to quality.	Some incentives to reduce costs through financial devolution.	Barriers to cross-disciplinary research and teaching.	High levels of access for qualified individuals.	Some incentive.	No effect	Some incentives and collaboration.	

n.a. not applicable.
Source: Country reports.

Table 3.2c. **Higher education financing schemes: government funding with low fees**

| Different types of schemes | Criteria for evaluating financing schemes |||||||
| | Efficiency ||| Equity | Generating new resources | Other criteria ||
	Increasing benefits	Decreasing costs	Other impacts on cost-effectiveness			Increasing participation	Generating new finance partnerships
Netherlands: Central government provides majority of funds for universities with some income from fees and contracts. Institutions currently funded on number of student years. Plans for introducing performance element. Higher vocational institutions already funded by input and output criteria.	Only weak incentives currently for quality in universities but more in Institutes of Higher Vocational Education	Weak incentives to reduce costs. Institutes of Higher Vocational Education with devolved budgets have incentives to reduce costs.	Positive incentive for not graduating students quickly in universities but not in Institutes of Higher Vocational Education.	High levels of access for qualified individuals.	Incentives for contract work.	Diversity of types encourages participation.	Some incentive to collaborate.

Source: Country reports.

are planned in three-year blocks but provided on a yearly basis, with separate elements for teaching and research. Funding for teaching is based on planned student enrolment numbers in different wprogrammme areas, with different weighting according to broad fields (*e.g.* humanities) for each full-time student year, with an additional annual performance target for each student.

In the Czech Republic, all universities are public and come directly under the Ministry of Education. These charge no fees and gain only a small amount of their revenues from private contract work. The majority of funding comes from central government, with separate grants for teaching and research from different ministries. Since 1990, universities have gained increasing financial autonomy with funding going to individual faculties since 1994. Government allocations are determined according to a variety of "normative" criteria which include performance elements.

In Austria, the universities and the *Fachhochschulen* are financed primarily by the federal government. The *Fachhochschulen* gain approval for courses from the *Fachhochschule* Council and are funded on a unit cost basis according to enrolments in different programme areas with different weightings. Course providers are obliged to carry out detailed cost accounting audited by the Science Ministry. Sources of income include *Bund* (54%), *Länder* government (36%); local authority (8%) and private funds (2%). The universities are also largely funded by the *Bund*, with *Länder* governments and local authorities contributing only through capital investments in buildings and facilities. Since 1990, a variety of reforms have been introduced which devolve financial responsibility and seek to improve efficiency and increase the transparency of cost accounting. Boards of trustees have been established which are responsible for development plans and allocation of staff budgets in consultation with the new university advisors who represent regional authorities and the social partners. The allocations of government funds for teaching are made according to the plan for the development and financing of the *Fachhochschule* sector, which relates to inter-university planning needs and planned student numbers.

Government funding with low fees

This model differs from the first model above in that the fee element of funding is relatively low.

In the Netherlands, tertiary education institutions receive some of their funds from fees and private contracts, but the vast majority from central government. The relative shares of funding for universities are: government (70%), fees (6%) and other private sources (24%). Higher vocational institutions receive a somewhat higher proportion from fees (16%) and a lower proportion from private contracts (13%) but a similar proportion from government (71%). Ninety per cent of government funds for tertiary education institutions are paid in a lump sum with the remaining 10% earmarked for specific purposes. Funding allocations for universities are now ("STABEK system") largely based on numbers of student years. A new performance based system (PBM) to be introduced in 2000 would provide greater incentives to quality with 50% of the teaching budgets dependent on the number of diplomas awarded, 13% on the number of new enrolments and the remaining 37% according to a fixed tariff.

Funding for learners

OECD countries have different means for funding student learning including self-funding and a variety of loans, grants and scholarships provided by central and regional governments. Public subsidies, in the form of grants and loans, vary in their form according to how far they are related to student and family means, how far they are dependent on merit or achievement, and the level at which they have to be repaid. Loans may be repaid in full or part, with or without interest, and over different time periods. In some cases, repayments are only due when graduates reach a certain income level and are phased through an income-related payment schedule. Both grants and loans may be made contingent on students achieving certain levels of performance throughout their study periods. Most countries make a number of different types of subsidy available with different eligibility criteria. The main consideration behind the design of these packages has generally been to ensure that students make a contribution commensurate with the benefits they gain from higher education, without placing investment burdens on students which would deter those who might benefit from studying, or which would impact unequally on students with different means and thus undermine equity in access. The main systems mentioned in the country reports are as follows.

Self-financing

Students incur costs in subsistence and accommodation, the purchase of books, materials and equipment, and fees. In most countries they make some contribution towards these from funds deriving from their families, from savings or from part-time earnings. However, the degree to which they contribute varies considerably. In Japan and South Korea, students self-finance the majority of their costs. In Japan, these can be as high as one million yen per year for fees in private universities, not to mention the costs of living expenses. Here it is estimated that the total expenses of study for the individuals are met from parental contributions (75%); part-time jobs (17.6%); and scholarships (5.7%).

Family allowances

In Austria, for example, there is an entitlement for students to receive family allowances until the age of 26.

Means-tested study grants

In Austria students are entitled to a grant dependent on income and achievement; in Norway students are entitled to a grant dependent on income when they do not live with their parents.

Performance-contingent grants

Students entering higher education in the Netherlands since September 1997 are entitled to a loan which converts into a grant if the student passes 50% of courses in each year and graduates in four years. In some instances (technical studies, medicine, studies with a large practical element) studies may take longer than four years, and therefore the entitlement period is longer also. Grants available to students in the Czech Republic are also dependent on achievement. Swedish students are entitled to grants during the programme for a maximum of twelve terms of study dependent on both their own income and achievement. The amount of study assistance is reduced if the student's own income exceeds a certain level. When first accepted for a study programme the student is entitled to study assistance for the first year, but to continue receiving this aid students must show sufficient achievement.

Interest-bearing loans

Loans schemes are available to students in many countries. In Sweden, loans are repayable by graduates at 4% of annual income. In Norway, interest on loans starts to accumulate after the student has completed his/her education. No payment is required until approximately ten months after interest begins to accumulate. The student receives a repayment plan which can cover a period of up to 15-20 years.

Scholarships

These are provided for students with particular levels of ability and need in Japan, Austria and elsewhere.

Other specific grants

These are intended for expenses such as travel, accommodation, subsistence and books and are available to students in particular categories in a number of countries.

The rationale for tertiary financing approaches

In all countries, necessarily both private and public resources contribute towards the financing of higher education. However, the relative share of the contributions by the state, individuals and by employers varies markedly between countries without

© OECD 2000

any apparent relation to the distribution of benefits. Distributions are determined by different national traditions with different priorities as regards expansion, equity, efficiency and public affordability.

Countries with very high levels of individual investment in tertiary education, such as Japan and South Korea, have benefited from the large contribution of private providers and investors and this has led to rapid expansion in enrolments, which would probably not have been affordable had finance depended largely on government. However, these gains have come at some cost in terms of equity and, in some cases, quality. Tertiary education institutions in these countries are clearly ranked and students with more personal financial resources have better access to the higher ranking and more expensive private universities, as well as the benefits of studying in the better public universities, without the necessity of spending long hours in paid work to meet their subsistence needs. The provision of scholarships has only partly mitigated these problems of inequity resulting from self-financing. Reliance on private investment has also caused under-resourcing of research in some universities and has thus led to a lowering of quality.

Countries with a high proportion of public investment in tertiary education have been able to avoid access to tertiary education becoming dependent on personal means, and have thus ensured that able students have received good quality education, although this has not necessarily made the social composition of recruitment to tertiary education anything like equitable. Moreover, pressures on public finance in these institutions have often enforced limitation on the expansion of tertiary education. Public perceptions that students are gaining disproportionate benefits in relation to their own contributions have re-enforced a climate where continued expansion cannot be funded without increased private contributions.

Greater emphasis on the necessary complementarity of public and private finance of tertiary education has led to significant net increases in resources. Universities in many countries have been increasingly encouraged to seek out private finance for research and consultancy activities, which in some cases now contribute as much as a third of total income. Where government funding for research is in part contingent upon the amount of private finance raised, this has further increased incentives in institutions for gaining income from private contract work. This has, of course, also had effects on the balance of different kinds of research conducted in universities, with increasing emphasis on applied and policy-relevant research which is best placed to generate additional funds.

Relationship between financing approaches, and equity and efficiency in tertiary education

High levels of private finance in the funding of tertiary education institutions have clearly helped to mobilise additional resources and, in some respects, to increase efficiency, although the effects on quality and equity have sometimes been less positive. Modes of allocating public funds have also had differential effects on efficiency and equity.

Traditional systems of funding tertiary education teaching costs through input measurement systems have sometimes had negative effects on quality and efficiency. Where universities and other institutions are competing with each other to enrol students, systems of *per capita* funding can be said to have both efficiency and quality incentives. Institutions will maximise surplus resources through increasing enrolments of students through teaching in efficient ways. They also need to have concern for quality since their reputations will have an effect on levels of student recruitment and income received. However, in some countries, institutions are not really competing for students, either because there is a tradition of local attendance or because places are allocated centrally. In these cases, there may still be incentives for efficiency, which may generate surpluses which can enhance staff conditions and maximise opportunities for undertaking desirable and prestige-enhancing activities like research and consultancy. However, the incentives towards quality in teaching may be weak. This is particularly the case in systems which fund institutions for each student year enrolment. In such cases, as in the Netherlands (under the "HOBEK" system of funding), universities actually had an incentive to enrol as many students as possible and to keep them as long as possible, without regard to their progress towards graduation. (Under the performance based – PBM – system that will be introduced in 2000, there will be less incentive to enrol as many students as possible.)

The need to improve quality in teaching and research has led to a number of countries adopting elements of performance-related funding. These systems normally make a portion of the total budget for teaching or research dependent on various outcome measures. For teaching, these have included criteria requiring students to pass a certain proportion of courses each year and to graduate within a specific period, as in the Netherlands and Sweden. Performance criteria for research funding have included measures of levels of research income from public and private sources, measures of success in research student study, and measures of publication rates and quality. Such systems may provide strong incentives for improving performance and quality, but may also present certain pitfalls. Making funding contingent upon student success in assessment can lead to institutions lowering standards, unless secure quality monitoring procedures are in place. Making research funding dependent on publication output can skew publishing strategies towards quantity rather than quality, if adequate systems for measuring quality are not in place. Likewise, incentives to encourage the raising of research funds from private contracts can reduce the incentives for research in non-applied and non-policy oriented fields.

Changes in funding mechanisms have often been accompanied by reforms which devolve greater financial responsibility down to the institutions themselves. This can have positive effects on motivation and efficiency at the institutional level. However,

© OECD 2000

these types of system also necessitate greater monitoring of institutional practices and performance. Enhanced quality control measures have inevitably increased the load of administrative work on staff in terms of accounting, documentation and data reporting, not to mention the additional time investments that have to be made for market research and marketing activities, where institutions also have autonomy in recruitment. Together with the additional activities involved in the reporting associated with performance-based funding systems, this means a considerable overall increase in transaction costs, which may offset some of the efficiency gains resulting from the reforms.

Similar dilemmas arise in terms of the funding of students. Many countries have sought to shift the burden of costs more towards the individual, as expansion has put intolerable strains on public finances. In practice, this has meant a shift from funding via non-contingent grants to funding through a combination of grants and loans which may be targeted, progress-dependent and income-contingent. There is little evidence to date that these forms of funding have had negative effects on net student enrolment or even equality of access, providing that fees have remained standardised and largely publicly subsidised. They have clearly helped to lever additional funding for tertiary education and to provide strong incentives to student performance, particular when they are made progress-contingent. However, they have not yet generated much consensus as to their equitability in terms of making payment commensurate with benefits. Most loan systems are based on standardised fees regardless of programme, and require graduates to pay back the full amount borrowed, although at different rates according to their income. This system ignores the fact that returns to tertiary education study vary markedly according to the line of study and the future occupation entered, and according to different social groups. Women and ethnic minority see far lower wage returns to tertiary education than men and major groups, but contribute the same amounts. However, more equitable and acceptable alternatives to this system have not yet found. Differential fee charging for different programmes might more equitably reflect both the real cost of different programmes and the likely wage returns to participating students. However, this system would inevitably provide barriers to access to some students and skew recruitment away from areas of national need. Graduate taxes which operate over fixed periods, thereby involving differential repayments according to income, may be more equitable but have yet to prove their political acceptability. Retrospective graduate taxes, imposed on all graduate earners who have received publicly subsidised tertiary education, may also be justified on equity grounds, but they are likely to prove even less politically acceptable.

Adult participation in lifelong learning

Adult participation is the most crucial and problematic area for the attainment of lifelong learning. It is here where the gaps between current and desirable levels of provision are greatest and where inequalities are most marked. It is also here where there are most difficulties in mobilising the necessary funds to finance lifelong learning. This is partly because of the sheer extent of the deficits, and partly because of the complexity of any analysis of the costs and benefits of current and alternative modes of funding. Relative to other sectors, adult education and training is generally rather poorly funded by the state, both in terms of support for providers and support for learners. Objectives are often poorly defined, quality monitoring is limited, and policy co-ordination is inherently problematic.

Adult education and training represents the most heterogeneous and segmented of the sectors considered in this report. It comprises, for our purposes, general adult education in formal settings, including vocational education, basic skills education and self-improvement or leisure education; labour market training for the unemployed and other special groups; and enterprise-based training, both formal and informal. Formal responsibility for these different areas of activity is absent in some countries, and in others is spread between education and labour ministries at the central government level, regional and municipal authorities at the lower government levels, and also, in some countries, employers and social partner organisations. Sources of funding are commensurately diverse. Generally speaking, employers provide most of the funds for enterprise-based training, with some government subsidies in the cases of training for apprentices and particular groups of employees, like those facing redundancy or needing retraining as a result of restructuring. Labour market training provision for the unemployed and hard-to-employ is usually funded by the state, although employers may be made to make certain contributions in countries with compulsory training levy systems. General adult education may be funded by the state, or by voluntary organisations, and often involves individual contributions through the payment of fees.

The very segmented nature of the sector causes a number of difficulties in mobilising investment. For the state there are difficulties in co-ordinating policies and the funding flows where so many different organisations and partners are involved and where the monitoring of quality and efficiency is so problematic. Defining objectives for learning provision is difficult when it involves large numbers of individuals with diverse needs learning in widely different circumstances. Measuring costs for the different areas of provision is difficult given the paucity of data on participation, unit costs of provision, and other costs through foregone earning, production and leisure time. Measuring benefits is no less difficult, given the diversity of objectives. Monetary benefits are hard to measure, and non-monetary benefits, though particularly significant in this sector, are both unmeasurable and hard to prioritise.

For individuals and companies there are equal problems in assessing costs and benefits, since future returns are unpredictable. Individuals may be loath to invest in adult education and training because they cannot assess the future benefits. If they are in work, they cannot be sure that their employers will reward them for their additional skills or qualifications or even that their employment will last long enough for them to realise a return. If out of work, they cannot be sure that their learning will culminate successfully in additional qualifications or that these qualifications will have value on the labour market sufficient to justify their investment. Employers find it equally difficult to evaluate costs and benefits. The costs of in-company training are hard to measure, since they involve the lost production of instructors and learners and damage done to equipment as well as direct costs. Benefits are hard to measure, since there are no adequate systems for evaluating productivity gains from increased employee skills, given the other factors involved in productivity enhancement and since poaching by other companies may, in any case, deprive the employer of the chance to realise benefits from investments in employee training. Generally speaking, employers are believed to gain most and risk least from investment in firm-specific occupational training. Employees risk least in investing in training in skills and qualifications which are portable and which may be taken elsewhere if unrewarded in their current employment. For all parties there is the recurrent problem of externalities. No one can be sure to capture all the returns for their investment and so each party may be prone to under-invest.

Despite all the problems of cost-benefit analysis, the general presumption is that both individuals and firms benefit from investment in education and training, which is why investment occurs. Exactly how much employers invest is not known, but it is estimated that in OECD countries they pay for about 30% of the actual current costs. Individuals also invest, but no country has adequate data to say who and how much.

The following discussion considers the funding of adult education and training in three areas (Tables 3.3a – 3.3d): adult general education, labour market training for the unemployed, and enterprise-based training.

Adult general education

Adult education outside the workplace is fairly diverse in OECD countries, although it does not necessarily consume a large proportion of public funding on education. It generally includes various forms of "second chance" education in basic skills and general secondary school subjects, as well as vocational education and what is broadly termed "leisure and community" education. Arrangements vary in different countries as to who provides and who funds each type. Frequently, secondary and basic skills, "remedial" or continuation education are provided in public institutions, organised at local level and funded jointly from central and local government revenues and partially from fees. Vocational education is often provided in both the public and private sectors, whilst leisure and community education are provided by municipal authorities and voluntary associations, with funding from the state, from associations and from individuals through fees. Public funding tends to be on the

© OECD 2000

Mobilising Financial Resources for Lifelong Learning

Table 3.3a. **Adult financing schemes: government-funded adult education**

Different types of schemes	Criteria for evaluating financing schemes							
	Efficiency			Equity	Generating new resources	Other criteria		
	Increasing benefits	Decreasing costs	Other impacts on cost-effectiveness			Increasing participation	Generating new finance partnerships
Danish Taximeter scheme	Encourages institutions to compete for students on basis of quality. Provides comparability between education and non-education-based learning.	Strong incentive to reduce costs to approved rate and further.	Periodic review of rates maintains pressure on ensuring cost-effectiveness.	Provides higher rates for programmes serving clients with severe needs in order to discourage "skimming".	Creates open-ended obligation for state to meet demand.	Encourages learner choice.	n.a.
Japanese adult education: Funded by municipalities with small fee element.	Weak incentives to quality.	Weak incentives to reduce costs.	None.	Regional inequalities due to different regional tax bases and infrastructures.	Small additional funds from fees.	Diversity of providers encourages participation.	No effect.
Swedish adult education: Adult education institutes funded from municipalities and fees. Folk high schools funded from central government grants and fees.	Weak incentives to quality.	Weak incentives to reduce costs.	n.a.	High level of largely free provision enhances equity.	Limited effect.	Diversity promotes high level participation.	State-voluntary sector partnerships.
Dutch ROCs: Largely funded from municipalities which are reimbursed by central government. Some fee charging and local tax contributions. Output-related element.	Performance criteria incentivise quality.	Economies of scale reduce costs.	n.a.	High level of access in each region.	Limited effect.	n.a.	Partnerships with employers for apprentice programmes

n.a. not applicable.
Source: Country reports.

© OECD 2000

Table 3.3b. **Adult financing schemes: private and voluntary sector provision**

Different types of schemes	Criteria for evaluating financing schemes							
	Efficiency			Equity	Generating new resources	Other criteria		Generating new finance partner-ships
	Increasing benefits	Decreasing costs	Other impacts on cost-effectiveness			Increasing participation	
Japan: Community Cultural Centres funded primarily from fees and private adult institutes funded entirely from fees.	Market incentives to improve quality.	Market incentives to reduce costs.	Little regulation may cause uneven effectiveness.	Access dependent on ability to pay.	Additional funding from fees and community sponsors.	Diversity of local provision encourages participation.	Brings in voluntary partners.
Norway: Study associations funded from central government and fees.	Market incentives to improve flexibility and quality.	Market incentives to reduce costs.	Positive effect on combining learning and work.	Broad access permitted by cost-sharing by individuals and government.	Additional funding from fees paid by individuals and other non-public sources.	n.a.	n.a.

n.a. not applicable.
Source: Country reports.

Mobilising Financial Resources for Lifelong Learning

Table 3.3c. **Adult financing schemes: incentives for individuals to invest in training**

| Different types of schemes | Criteria for evaluating financing schemes |||||||
| | Efficiency ||| Equity | Generating new resources | Other criteria ||
	Increasing benefits	Decreasing costs	Other impacts on cost-effectiveness			Increasing participation	Generating new finance partner-ships
Tax-exemption for personal learning costs: Italy and the Netherlands.	n.a.	n.a.	n.a.	Lowest benefits to those most likely to be excluded from training.	Encourages private investment.	Encourages participation.	n.a.
Employer and government funded paid training leave: Austria, Italy, Norway and the Netherlands.	Does not incentivise individual to make good use of leave.	No effects.	n.a.	Encourages training amongst excluded groups – depending on eligibility.	Promotes individual investment.	Encourages participation.	n.a.

n.a. not applicable.
Source: Country reports.

Table 3.3d. Adult financing schemes: incentives to employers

Different types of schemes	Criteria for evaluating financing schemes							
	Efficiency			Equity	Generating new resources	Other criteria		
	Increasing benefits	Decreasing costs	Other impacts on cost-effectiveness			Increasing participation	Generating new finance partner-ships	
Tax exemptions for employer training: Finland and the Netherlands.	No effects.	No effects.	n.a.	No incentives for employers to distribute training opportunities equitably.	Promotes employer investment in training.	May not broaden participation.	No effects.
Training levies: Italy, Korea and the Netherlands.	No incentives to quality.	No incentives to reduce costs except where levy only partly reimburses costs as in the Netherlands.	Can encourage wasteful training expenses. Problems with threshold for participation due to small employer resistance to participation.	Encourages suitable share of training costs between firms. May not promote equity in individual access to training, although compulsory levies in the Netherlands are often distributed on equity criteria.	Promotes employer investment.	Promotes more training although not always maximum diffusion.	No effects except through inter-firm training schemes
Targeted government funding for employer training: the Netherlands, Italy Sweden	Quality incentives can be built in.	n.a.	External efficiency gains: can steer investment to areas of national priority.	Can provide levers for steering training to excluded groups.	Can promote employer investment.	n.a.	State-firm partnership.

n.a. not applicable.
Source: Country reports.

basis of full-time equivalent student numbers without any performance element. Fee levels vary considerably according to type of provider and type of programme. The following are some examples from the country reports.

Fees in adult education

In Japan, adult general education is provided by local education boards with funds from fees and central and local government sources (80% local). There are also private Community Cultural Centres funded predominantly from fees and private adult education institutes funded entirely through fees. Employers also sometimes fund employees on post-graduate courses and the government runs some schemes to subsidise employees in general education programmes outside the workplace (*e.g.* self-improvement for older workers).

In Sweden, most adult education is funded by the municipalities. Popular adult education is provided in the Folk High Schools and in adult education institutions funded by fees and central government grants through the Council for Popular Adult Education. Public loans for living, buying study materials, etc., are available to most of the students in adult education.

In the Netherlands, ROCs and schools provide adult vocational and secondary general education respectively. These activities are funded largely by local authorities from central government grants and, to a smaller extent, from fees and local taxes. Central government funding accounts for 72% of total funding for adult basic education and 91% for adult general secondary education.

In Denmark, most of the direct costs of adult education and training are borne by the state, through the taximeter payments and other forms of institutional support (Box 3.1). Direct costs are paid to a lesser extent, by individuals and enterprises. For example, 60% of the Folk High Schools' revenues come from the state, with the balance from individuals and private companies. Student fees pay 20-40% of the costs for Open Education courses. In the adult vocational training programmes operated by labour market authorities, the share paid by enterprises for their employees ranges from nothing, for training that uses standard courseware, to 100% for training that uses tailor-made curricula. Where a trainee allowance is paid by the state (in cases where training leave for employed workers is not paid), the employer pays a share calculated in the same way (up to 100% for tailor made courses).

Funding for general adult education is often precarious. It tends to receive low priority in central government education budgets and local funding can be subject to the vagaries of local government financial situations (*e.g.* the current financial strains in some municipalities in Japan). Public funding systems often lack efficiency incentives and there tend to be few mechanisms for monitoring the quality or benefits of adult education provision. In many countries, there is a plethora of voluntary associations providing different kinds of education and cultural activity with relatively little

© OECD 2000

Box 3.1. **Danish taximeter system**

After a few years of experience with the taximeter scheme, there are a number of issues that arise:

- *The open-ended nature of the taximeter obligations.* Because the taximeter payments are guaranteed to approved institutions as long as they enrol students, it is possible in principle, for them to enrol large numbers of persons, without limit. To reduce budget uncertainty, the authorities agreed that as from 1999, a reserve of 1-2% of the total allocation for the scheme would be set aside to cover unforeseen surges in enrolments.
- *Inefficiencies arising from the gap between the actual cost of provision and the amount reimbursed by the taximeter scheme.* The taximeter scheme provides an incentive to providers to improve the efficiency of their programmes, by allowing them to retain any excess in taximeter rates over the actual costs, and forcing them to pay any costs in excess of the taximeter rates. If, on the one hand, the taximeter rates are adjusted too frequently to take account of efficiency gains, providers may have reduced incentive to pursue efficiency-enhancing innovations. If, on the other hand, taximeter rates are adjusted too slowly, there may be a loss in overall efficiency of the total expenditures to the extent that some providers continue to use less efficient methods. Although the ministry has no intention of recapturing the "profits" realised by those institutions whose actual costs are below the taximeter rates, there may be some adjustment in the rates to improve overall efficiency of the system.

The taximeter scheme is an example of a fiscal tool for improving efficiency and cost-effectiveness of lifelong learning. Here are other, non-fiscal strategies that seem to push in the same direction:

- *Recognition of training outcomes.* The Ministry of Labour's main training programmes (*De Kompetencegivende Uddannelser og Særaktiviteter*) provide certificated training results. This means that the results are visible to employers and individuals alike. In contrast, many of the Ministry of Education programmes (outside the area of adult vocational training) do not lead to certificates, except in the case where individuals complete requirements for a formal education degree or diploma. Many activities are expressly intended to serve broader, non-vocational purposes.
- *Involvement of social partners in deciding curricula and outcome measures.* Education as well as labour market programmes involve social partners extensively in the process of deciding what courses to offer, developing curriculum and assessment practices, and, often, in the actual delivery of programmes. This increases the acquired skills and competencies are up-to-date and relevant to labour market needs.
- *High degree of individual choice.* Because of the range of well-developed, highly accessible learning opportunities that cater to varied education backgrounds, learning styles, and learning objectives, it seems relatively easy for individuals to find "a place" in the system.

Mobilising Financial Resources for Lifelong Learning

> Box 3.1. **Danish taximeter system** (*cont.*)
>
> It is difficult to observe whether or how much these features actually improve the effectiveness or quality of learning opportunities, or what would have happened in their absence. Scattered evidence is mixed. Immediate impacts on employability seem debatable. Statistics on the labour market training programmes show that, in 1995, only slightly more than a quarter of participants who were unemployed when they started the programme, were employed after completing it. The Educational Leave programme does not seem to be major resource for unemployed or poorly qualified persons trying to re-qualify themselves. Only 14% of participants between January 1994 and April 1995 were unemployed; though persons lacking formal vocational qualifications comprise two-fifths of the labour force, they comprise only a fifth of the employed persons participating in training. Finally, the educational leave programme evidently is considerably less appealing to private employers than to public employers: private enterprises were less than half as likely as public enterprises to send persons on training leave. Yet these statistics belie considerable support for the programme. For example, though nearly half of those who participated in the educational leave programme reported substantial monetary loss during participation, only 5% said they were dissatisfied with the training leave. Nearly 90% indicated they would take leave again. Three-fourths expressed satisfaction with the professional development that occurred, four-fifths with the personal development that occurred. And these results were found despite the fact that relatively few (1/3 or less) were given more interesting work, had greater job security, or expected higher wages. On the part of employers, the vast majority thought that training leave would be of benefit in the long run (60% of private enterprises, 76% of public employers), and that they would conclude new agreements in the future (70 and 85% respectively) [Andersen *et al.* (1996)].

co-ordination which reduces overall efficiency, although it may widen participation. There is also a very low level of integration between adult provision and the schools sector, despite the obvious potential for common use of facilities and staff. The sector as a whole tends to rank low in terms of equality of access, particularly as regards self-improvement or leisure-oriented education, since access here often depends on the ability to pay. Whereas adult education can have considerable social benefits, in terms of social inclusion and community building, it is often the most socially marginal who have least access to it. Some countries, however, such as the Nordic states, do have strong traditions of adult education. In Denmark, for instance, most persons participate in adult education and training programmes, such as open education and adult liberal education, on their own. Thus they give up their free time to participate, though often such participation is viewed as a form of leisure. Indirect costs, in the form of foregone income, are paid to a large extent by individuals. (Poorly qualified

© OECD 2000

employees are eligible to receive support payments equal to the maximum unemployment benefit, for a time that varies according to the vocational nature of the courses and whether they qualify adults for further study.)

Labour market training for the unemployed

Most countries provide a variety of special schemes to enhance the employability and employment of the adult unemployed. These range from information and guidance services to programmes for retraining, skills enhancement and job search. Funding systems for these are not systematically covered in the country reports, but it is safe to say that most of the funding comes from central government sources, albeit from different ministerial budgets. Research suggests very variable returns to these schemes in terms of future employment. In general, there is a grave lack of data on cost-benefits in this area of provision.

Lifelong learning and enterprise-based training

Levels of financing for enterprise-based training vary considerably between different countries, although inadequate country data and incomparable national definitions and measures make precise estimates of differences difficult. Incidence and intensity of training also vary significantly within countries. National research studies tend to suggest that training is more prevalent in larger companies than smaller companies and in certain sectors rather than others. Those benefiting most from in-company training tend to be those already better qualified and in more senior positions. Women tend to receive less in-company training than men, and temporary and part-time workers less than permanent and full-time workers.

A number of measures have been put in place by national authorities to increase the availability of financial resources for lifelong learning that is undertaken in connection with work. Some are centred on individuals.

Tax incentives to individual learners

In the Netherlands, individuals can deduct vocational education and training expenses from personal taxation. Italy also has tax incentives for individuals engaged in training either as learners or tutors. These tax incentives tend to benefit the better paid who are most likely to be engaged in training anyway.

Employment leave for training

Italy has regulations allowing paid leave of absence for training for certain employees. Austrian regulations entitle those with three years or more in a company the right to up to 12 months unpaid study leave with the government contributing an allowance of ATS 5 600 per month. In the Netherlands, government funds have

© OECD 2000

recently become available to finance unpaid training leave. In Japan, around 20% of employers claim to offer paid training leave for some employees.

Other regulations are aimed at enterprises.

Tax benefit schemes

In the Netherlands, employers receive tax exemption for training as well as exemption from VAT for training activities. Hungary provides tax allowances for non-profit making organisation engaged in educational services. In addition, Finland has proposed that a proportion of company taxation should be used to ensure training even in times of recession.

Levies

The Netherlands has voluntary levies in about 60 sectors. These are allocated to sectoral training funds which subsidise training by employers. They are mostly paid by employers and usually as a proportion of payroll (average 0.5%). Training funds do not fully cover the costs of training and so leave an incentive for efficiency for employers engaged in training. In Korea, employers are obliged to pay into funds for the promotion of training. Italy also imposes levies for training. Levy schemes have been criticised because they may encourage inefficient and inappropriate training, and because it can be difficult to agree on the level of levy and the company size threshold at which companies are included. However, they have the advantage of spreading the load for funding training between employers and thus mitigating the externalities problem.

Targeted government subsidies for in-company training

In Sweden, the state subsidises companies for training where needs arise out of restructuring; where there is a labour market need over and above the specific need of that company; or where workers need re-training prior to redundancy. There are also state subsidies for training in small firms. Italy provides state subsidies to companies in the south.

New measures proposed in the various countries include the following. Austria has proposed new measures for funding further training for gifted apprentices. These include state grants for up to 50% of the costs of training to master craftsman level for those in or contemplating self-employment. Other subsidies of 50% would be available for those undertaking training abroad and of 33% for those undertaking higher training at work. Sweden is proposing to introduce new forms of action planning for young people seeking to make choices about future training and career courses. Recent legislation in Italy proposes new measures to co-ordinate the supply of training and to achieve greater integration between adult and school provision. New consumer taxes (*e.g.* for environmental damage) are proposed as additional sources of funds for training and new personal training accounts as ways of incentivising individual investment. These would be accounts of both funds and time invested in training for individuals, with part of the resources deposited by government, firms and individuals available to individuals to spend on training and self-improvement (the UK Government has made similar proposals for Individual Learning Accounts, funded jointly by individuals, firms and the state). Italy also proposes a 5% levy on the wages of temporary workers to go into a training fund set up by the Ministry of Labour and Social Security.

Conclusions

The preceding chapter examined ways to strengthen the incentives to invest in lifelong learning. This chapter has focused on mechanisms to provide the financial resources that can be used to put those incentives to work. It has considered whether *existing* financing mechanisms provide a sound platform for initiatives to expand public resources for lifelong learning, and to facilitate private financing, while strengthening incentives to improve efficiency, and achieving equitable balance between who pays and who benefits. In the initial education sector, a number of countries pursue equity and efficiency objectives by raising money through central governments, and spending it through lower levels of government where programmatic decisions are made. They follow a general trend towards devolving decisions about funding by giving regional authorities greater autonomy in allocating resources and institutions greater autonomy in spending them. This is true in different ways across a range of countries that includes Austria, the Czech Republic, Italy, Norway, the Netherlands and Sweden. Even in Japan and South Korea, with traditionally centralised control of funding, debates have begun about giving institutions increased autonomy in their use of resources. The objectives behind these changes have generally been to increase efficiency by giving more incentives to local managers and staff and by bringing decision-making closer to operational realities. The changes may also seek to raise efficiency through stimulating increased competition between institutions, although this does not go beyond the creation of limited or quasi markets in any current examples. In most cases it is too early to judge what the effects of these reforms have been on cost efficiency and there is equally little evidence in relation to effects on quality. The logic that competitive institutional funding systems leads to expansion and reduced unit costs follows providing there is scope and demand for expansion and providing that additional transaction costs do not outweigh other efficiency gains. The effects on quality and equity, even where performance measures are built in to incentivise these, would seem to be far less predictable.

Currently it would appear that in many countries individuals significantly underinvest in tertiary education. There is a common feeling that individuals who realise lifetime earnings gains of between 50 and 100% (as until recently in Korea) through higher education should be prepared to meet more of the costs. The difficulty lies in finding systems to make feasible higher individual investment, that are seen as equitable and which do not damage equality of access. Graduate taxes have the potential to lever considerable additional resources without having restrictive effects on access. However, beneficiaries of publicly-funded tertiary education will have to be convinced that they should pay back in taxes sums commensurate with the benefits they have gained.

Employer and employee under-investment in work-related lifelong learning is being tackled in scattered ways such as more favourable tax treatment of training expenditures, as well as levies that mandate outlays. Comprehensive policies and practices are lacking, however. Finally, in terms of the funding arrangements for the whole system of post-compulsory education, there is a need to explore new ways of increasing the co-ordination and coherence of funding systems. Funding regimes in the sector as a whole are extremely diverse and often lack transparency and concerted planning and this reduces their overall efficiency. Greater co-ordination between different participating government ministries, different levels of government and other social partners is essential also to ensure that financing mechanisms reinforce long-term effectiveness and efficiency.

Finally, there are scattered signs that the mandate for lifelong learning is leading to a fundamental reallocation of existing resources across functional areas of existing education and training systems. In Sweden, for example, responsibility for basic education for poorly qualified adults has been shifted from labour market programmes to education programmes. In the majority of OECD countries, demographic trends work in favour of lower outlays for foundation education. This theoretically means that it would be possible to move resources away from foundation education and towards adult education, for example. But it is not occurring. Reasons include desire in many countries to take advantage of demographic trends to improve achievements in foundation education by increasing teacher/pupil ratios. There is also a difficulty in simply seeing teachers and other education personnel, who constitute the greatest single cost in all sectors in all countries, as flexible commodities. Moreover, in many countries, there is a desire to reduce total budgets rather than to re-deploy resources.

© OECD 2000

Chapter 4

What Next?

The vision of a learning society, where lifelong learning for all is seen as both necessary and desirable, commands considerable consensus across OECD countries. There is real enthusiasm for the concept and a political recognition that the objectives laid out in the OECD Report *Lifelong Learning for All* (OECD, 1996) provide a useful guide for future developments. Countries differ widely, however, with respect to the extent that they have articulated specific objectives, and put in place strategies for realising unmet goals.

The challenge of this report and the country studies on which it is based, has been to help move the debates about lifelong learning beyond statements about goals, to more focused discussion of strategies, priorities, and means. They have done this by introducing questions about resource implications and how to address the constraints they impose on the choice of options facing governments, employers, and individuals.

This chapter provides a brief summary of the more common measures individual OECD countries are taking to address the issue of affordability, looks at further measures they might take, and suggests how the OECD might support them in this task.

The issue of affordability

Affordability of lifelong learning is a live issue for all the OECD countries that contributed to this report. This is despite their very different starting points, with regard to the levels of qualifications of the population, current participation in learning activities and different national objectives for lifelong learning.

The issue raises three questions:

– What is meant by lifelong learning, who is to be included and involved, and what is it likely to cost (Chapter 1)?

– How can the cost-effectiveness and quality of provision and learning be improved, and the benefits enhanced, thereby raising the rates of return to

© OECD 2000

lifelong learning and strengthening the incentives of different actors to invest in lifelong learning (Chapter 2)?
- How can the financing mechanisms that enable various actors to invest in lifelong learning be strengthened so as to enable them to allocate additional resources (Chapter 3)?

The following summarises the results of the country studies with respect to these three questions (see also the tables in Annexes 2 and 3).

How ambitious a goal have countries set, and how costly will it be to achieve?

There is no common understanding among OECD countries of what lifelong learning includes, and there are different national priorities at any particular point in time. For some, such as Finland and Sweden, lifelong learning begins with nursery education and extends to all types of adult learning throughout life. Similarly, in Japan, there is an emphasis on a broad holistic view of lifelong learning that starts with foundation education and embraces all forms of formal and informal adult learning. In Japan, the concept of lifelong learning is seen as having the potential to transform the school-centred education system. Other countries, such as Austria and Hungary, appear at present to be concentrating more on improving formal upper secondary and tertiary education and adult vocational education and training.

Not only do OECD countries place emphasis on different aspects of lifelong learning, they also have quite different starting points in relation to the development of policy and objectives in this area. Five of the countries contributing to this report currently have a well-developed national strategy for lifelong learning that includes all sectors and all ages, and many others are working towards this. In several countries, objectives for lifelong learning, particularly in terms of concrete targets for participation in education and training, have either just been formulated or are still in the process of formulation. The idea of viewing the whole education and training system through the lens of lifelong learning is still, therefore, relatively new to many OECD countries.

Most countries are not yet at the stage of fully translating their goals into operational targets, such as the indicative targets for participation in lifelong learning calculated by the Secretariat in 1996 (see Annex 1). Where they have formulated targets, they are tailored to particular needs and the nature of existing institutional arrangements. Regardless of how far countries have progressed in establishing operational targets, they stress the importance of establishing targets with respect to quality, as well as quantity.

Thus, lifelong learning as it is taking shape, is not merely symbolic, even where operational objectives are not clearly specified. For most of the countries covered by this report, the lifelong learning mandate represents significant net new resource requirements. Crude estimates, where they have been made, imply annual additional costs on the order of 2-4% of GDP – somewhat more than the earlier Secretariat estimates.

Strengthening incentives to invest in lifelong learning: how can efficiency and cost-effectiveness be improved, and benefits increased?

Given the resource requirements of the various configurations of lifelong learning, it is unlikely that governments simultaneously can pay the full costs and ensure that all demand for lifelong learning is satisfied. But if non-governmental actors – employers and individuals, in particular – are to pay, the expected rates of return need to be high enough to give them a stronger incentive to invest. Raising rates of return depend, in turn, on increasing the expected benefits of various forms of lifelong learning, and reducing their costs. In this regard, the OECD countries contributing to this report place the greatest emphasis on increasing the efficiency and cost effectiveness in provision of education and training.

Reducing costs

Measures vary from country to country and are considered in some detail in Chapter 2. One is a process of rationalisation and reorganisation of education and training provision taking place at a national level in a number of OECD countries. This process usually has been driven by fiscal constraints and pressures to "do more with less". But it has had the positive spin-off of encouraging different parts of education and training systems to seek out complementary partnerships and linkages, thereby allowing a more holistic approach to meeting client needs.

Most frequently mentioned are sector-specific measures which education and training providers are taking themselves to improve the efficiency education and training delivery. These include reducing the range of courses or programmes on offer in certain institutions or localities; rethinking modes of delivery to provide more flexible entry and exit points for learners; and, encouraging collaboration between different providers to cut programme development costs and to make more effective use of accommodation and equipment. There is considerable interest in expanding use of information and communications technology (ICT) to increase cost-effectiveness and, at the same time, widen access to lifelong learning opportunities. Chapter 2 includes case study examples of the type of developments in a number of OECD countries. The hoped-for efficiency gains of ICT are diminished by the potentially high initial financial outlay associated with some use of ICT, the lack of skilled teachers and instructors in many countries and the possibility of inequitable learner access to learning opportunities. As part of another approach to improving efficiency, there is increased attention being given to developing and using systems of assessment and recognition of acquired skills and competences (discussed further below) in

© OECD 2000

order to signal better prior learning, and to thereby avoid unnecessary education and training.

Increasing benefits

Raising expected rates of return – thereby strengthening incentives to invest in lifelong learning – depends as well on increasing benefits to lifelong learning. Efforts to improve quality of learning outcomes can be viewed as part of a larger strategy for increasing benefit. "Quality", however, is subjective to a certain degree, depending on expectations of learners and others, such as employers. In this regard, many countries are improving quality by devolving decision making from national levels, to levels closer to point of delivery in part to ensure that delivery methods and outcomes are more responsive to client needs and expectations.

However, in order to ensure that quality criteria are not entirely dependent on local needs and to make it easier to apply quality criteria across institutional settings, national authorities are taking a strong role in establishing frameworks for quality assurance. Some countries (Denmark, Hungary and Sweden, for example) plan to establish one body to cover all sectors; others (the Czech Republic, for example) are establishing separate bodies within particular sectors.

In addition to using output standards, national governments are pursuing other strategies for improving and ensuring quality of lifelong learning opportunities:

- One is to build the infrastructure for a system of lifelong learning. This includes development of systems for assessment and recognition of skills and competences, regardless of where they are acquired, so as to validate lifelong learning that occurs in formal education settings, as well as in the community, at home, or in the workplace. Improving infrastructure for lifelong learning also includes simplifying the pathways between different sectors.

- Systems of assessment and recognition of skills and competences are also seen as improving benefits of lifelong learning by increasing the portability of skills and competences between jobs, and between education settings and the workplace.

- Another is to focus more narrowly on ensuring that pressures to improve efficiency in provision, do not impact negatively on quality at point of deliver. In some countries (Austria and Finland), there is a commitment to continuation of public subsidies as a way of ensuring that quality is not sacrificed. In other countries, such as the Netherlands, the governmental role is to ensure quality of learning in public and private institutions by monitoring outcomes.

© OECD 2000

Putting incentives to work: how can financial resources be mobilised?

Strong incentives to invest, in the form of high social or private rates of return to lifelong learning, are not enough to ensure that lifelong learning is affordable. There also is a need for governmental authorities to exercise flexibility in allocating existing public resources in a way that will maximise lifelong learning, as well as financing mechanisms that allow individuals and employers to pay today for learning that generates benefits in the future.

There are limited signs of progress in financing mechanisms that would favour lifelong learning. On the public side, there is no clear indication in any of the country reports that a fundamental reallocation of resources is occurring as part of a deliberate attempt to achieve lifelong learning goals. In the majority of OECD countries, demographic trends are working in favour of lower outlays for foundation education. This theoretically means that it would be possible to move resources away from foundation education and towards adult education, for example. But it is not occurring:

- Many countries are trying to take advantage of demographic trends to improve achievements in foundation education by increasing teacher/pupil ratios.
- Though education staff constitute the greatest single cost in all sectors in all countries, it often is difficult to reallocate teachers and other education personnel across sectors because of qualifications required may be different.
- In many countries, there is already a concern about the high cost of education and training budgets in the current economic climate and there is therefore a desire to reduce total budgets rather than to re-deploy resources.
- There is lacking effective institutional arrangements for evaluating learning needs across different age groups of the population, and (re)allocating resources across ministerial portfolios.

Although public financing arrangements do not show signs of changing in ways that would lead to reallocation of net new resources towards lifelong learning, they do show signs of changing in ways that deliberately aim to reinforce cost effectiveness of current spending. There is a common move to devolve responsibility for budget decisions increasingly to the level of the provider in order to encourage providers to use their budgets more efficiently and, in some cases, to compete for students with other providers in a locality. Several countries are also experimenting with forms of output-related funding in order to increase both efficiency and quality of provision.

These funding mechanisms to cut costs, either simply by making providers more aware of and accountable for the real costs of education and training, or by encouraging the development of a quasi-market in education and training, may be effective initially. There is, however, a potential price to pay in terms of equality of access, particularly in relation to traditionally excluded groups, who may be more costly to edu-

© OECD 2000

cate and may be vulnerable in a competitive marketplace. Unless funding mechanisms are carefully and sensitively constructed, there may also be a loss of quality associated with some efficiency measures, which could have an overall negative effect on cost-effectiveness. Moreover, the greater the level of devolved responsibility for budgets and the greater the incentives are for providers to manipulate budgets to achieve specific outcomes, the greater becomes the likelihood of introducing potentially damaging distortions into the equation.

Financing mechanisms to assist individuals are well established in some countries in the formal education sector, particularly at the tertiary level. As fees are low or negligible in most of the countries covered, they take the form of allowances, means-tested study grants, performance-contingent, interest-bearing loans (often with below-market rates), and scholarships. In countries such as Japan and Korea where tuition charges can be high, these various instruments may cover direct costs as well as living costs and incidental expenses. Financing arrangements for adult learning are less developed. To the extent they exist, there are more variations in their generosity and coverage. Most tend to focus on replacing salary during training. They range from nearly full salary replacement to more modest allowances in lieu of salary. Some employers in some countries provide paid training leave. But coverage is highly variable, difficult to substantiate and generally non-mandatory.

There still are few financial mechanisms to enable individuals to undertake the cost of lifelong learning themselves. Individuals in the Netherlands can now deduct from pre-tax income the costs of participating vocational education and training. This is in contrast to the usual situation in which individuals pay costs out of after-tax income. A more radical proposal, under consideration in Italy, would allow individuals to place pre-tax income in individual training accounts to which employers and the state could also contribute.

With regard to employers, there are a few cases of mechanisms to make it easier for them to finance lifelong learning by lowering the cost of capital. In the Netherlands, for example, employers are allowed to deduct from pre-tax earnings more than 100% of certain training costs. Various levy grants schemes which tax employers if they do not train, effectively reduce the cost to firms of capital employed for training, by reducing to zero the opportunity costs for funds below the threshold. The more common approach is for the state to bear at least some of the costs to firms through training allowances to individuals and/or provision some forms of training that are state-subsidised.

From marginal change to paradigm shift

Developing a lifelong learning system for all will demand a considerable cultural shift in the way OECD countries think about directly financing education, training, and other learning opportunities, and in the way that they treat a wide range of issues that affect indirectly the affordability of lifelong learning. It appears from the country reports examined here that there is a genuine will to make this kind of cultural shift. Clearly, because individual OECD countries have to work within their own national contexts, the measures which each takes to make this kind of cultural shift will be different. However, there are three major areas where OECD could play a role in supporting individual countries in achieving this goal:

- Despite the detailed descriptions of efficiency and cost-reducing measures contained in many of the country reports, there is very little indication of their effects. There is clearly a need for further research into the effects of these measures in order to establish their contribution to making lifelong learning more affordable in OECD countries.

- There is a lack of data on the volume, place, and nature of learning opportunities because of the non-formal settings in which much learning occurs, and the fact that responsibilities for lifelong learning are fragmented among ministerial portfolios and policies. If public authorities and social partners are to address issues related to the affordability of lifelong learning and, more generally, monitor the progress in implementation of lifelong learning, there is need for concerted action to fill these data gaps.

- There also is an acute lack of data on the average and marginal costs of different forms of teaching and learning, provided in different settings, for different populations. The most commonly available data related to costs, those based on outlays and numbers of participants, are no substitute. In order to provide a sound base for evaluating the potential impact of policy alternatives on efficiency, there is need for building up a base of such data, from the service delivery level.

The OECD could work with Member countries in identifying possible sources of such data and resolving some of the measurement difficulties that arise.

There is a need to encourage OECD countries to develop a co-ordinated national strategy for lifelong learning which fully integrates questions of financing and affordability alongside other considerations. Such a strategy might include:

- Rethinking the roles and responsibilities of all the partners involved in providing opportunities for lifelong learning.

- Co-operation between relevant national government department (*e.g.* education, labour, social security, sport and leisure, health).

- Devising a staged strategy for reaching participation targets (established by national authorities, or, in the absence of such targets, targets formulated by the Secretariat) and ensuring that there is a focus on quality as well as quantity.

© OECD 2000

- Monitoring approaches to improve the transparency and recognition of knowledge, skills and competences acquired in lifelong learning.
- Monitoring progress towards better signalling the economic value of lifelong learning as an investment to enterprises, individuals, and third party sources of financing.
- Collecting and disseminating comprehensive and up-to-date information about the type of education and training which is taking place, current and future qualification and participation rates and trends and the unit costs of different types of education and training.
- Developing a stronger social partnership approach to education and training in the workplace and promoting more coherent links between learning and work.

Bibliography

ANDERSEN, D., APPELDORN, A. and WEISE, H. (1996),
Evaluation of the Danish Leave Schemes, Summary Report, Ministry of Labour, Copenhagen, August.

OECD (1995),
Literacy, Economy and Society: Results of the First International Adult Literacy Survey, Paris.

OECD (1996),
Lifelong Learning for All, Paris.

OECD (1997),
Literacy Skills for the Knowledge Society: Further Results from the International Adult Literacy Survey, Paris.

OECD (1999),
Education Policy Analysis, Paris.

OECD (2000),
Literacy in the Information Age: Final Report of the International Adult Literacy Survey, Paris.

Annex 1
Estimating Lifelong Learning Gaps

Credible estimates of resource requirements depend on having a clear idea of starting points, end-goals, and the operational objectives that need to be achieved along the way.

There are particular problems in formulating sound lifelong learning policies because of the difficulty of evaluating "learning deficits" (the past and future problems that lifelong learning is intended to address). How does one determine whether individuals or population groups are "lifelong learners"? Is it possible to establish operational objectives for public policy when some much of lifelong learning occurs beyond the reach of public institutions and policy?

When it launched the debate about lifelong learning at the January 1996 meeting of OECD Education Ministers, the Secretariat opened the discussion about resources with the question "by how much would existing institutional arrangements have to expand in order to achieve lifelong learning goals?" For the sake of discussion, the Secretariat estimated learning gaps on the basis of difference between *actual* participation rates in different components of formal and non-formal learning, and a number of different *target* participation rates, with the targets reflecting more and less ambitious visions of lifelong learning. The costs of closing these gaps were estimated on the basis of past costs of different forms of education and training. The purpose of the exercise was not to develop firm estimates of the costs of closing such learning gaps. Rather it was to focus discussion on discrete strategies that influence how affordable lifelong learning is to ministries of education: specifying goals that are more or less ambitious; reducing costs of learning; or shifting part of the financing burden to other ministries, and/or to the private sector (OECD, 1996, pp. 223-267; for additional estimates under different policy scenarios see OECD, 1999, pp. 7-26).

While recognising diverse possible interpretations of lifelong learning, deficits were defined in terms of shortcomings in education attainment levels, and objectives were defined in terms of increases in participation in formal as well as non formal learning.

To facilitate international comparison, the OECD defined attainment and participation with reference to ISCED (International Standard Classification of Educational Development) levels and literacy levels.

The ISCED levels are broken down as follows:

– ISCED 0: pre-school (early childhood development activities typically occurring before age 5 or 6).
– ISCED 1: the early years of compulsory education (typically occurring between the ages 5 or 6, and 12).
– ISCED 2: lower secondary education (typically the last years of compulsory education/training, occurring between the ages of 12 and 15 or 16).

- ISCED 3: upper secondary education (typically the first years of post-compulsory education, occurring between the ages of 15 or 16, and 17-19).

- ISCED 5: non-university education (typically involving up to two years of instruction; often culminating in a degree or certificate).

- ISCED 6: initial university education (typically 3-4 years of study culminating in a first university degree, such as a bachelors degree).

- ISCED 7: advanced university education (typically 1-3 years beyond the first university degree, culminating in a masters or doctorate degree).

Literacy levels refer to the measures used in the International Adult Literacy Survey. These levels are measured in three domains:

- Prose literacy: the knowledge and skills needed to understand and use information from texts, including editorials, news stories, poems and fiction.

- Document literacy: the knowledge and skills required to locate and use information contained in various formats, including job applications, payroll forms, transportation schedules, map, table and graphics.

- Quantitative literacy: the knowledge and skills required to apply arithmetic operations, either alone or sequentially, to numbers embedded in printed materials, such as balancing a cheque book, figuring out a tip, completing an order form, or determining the amount of interest on a loan from an advertisement.

Literacy levels range from 1 to 5; level 2 is frequently described as the threshold of "functional literacy", the bare minimum for most employment. There is a relatively strong correlation between literacy level 1 and ISCED 0/1; literacy level 2 and ISCED 2; literacy level 3 and ISCED 3; literacy levels 3/4/5 and ISCED 5; literacy levels 4/5 and ISCED 6/7.

Using these proxy measures, the Secretariat used the following participation benchmark targets for foundation learning as the basis for estimating *participation gaps* that had to be closed in order to implement the lifelong learning mandate:

- 90% of 18 year-olds to complete upper secondary education or equivalent apprenticeship training (ISCED level 3).

- 25% of 30 year-olds to have completed a non-university tertiary programme.

- 30% of 30 year-olds to have completed a short university degree programme (ISCED level 5).

- 13% of 30 year-olds to have completed a long university degree programme (ISCED level 6).

- 20% of poorly qualified adults (with an educational level of ISCED level 2 or below) to participate in basic adult education each year.

- 100% participation of long-term unemployed adults in retraining programmes each year.

- 40% of employees to participate in job-related training courses each year.

© OECD 2000

Annex 2
Estimates of Participation Gaps

Table A2.1. **Austria – All educational sectors**
(data for late 1990s)

Level/Sector	Relevant age cohort (yearly average)	Graduation rate (%)	Target percentage	Gap
Upper secondary[1]	15-19 year-olds (458 689)	79.8	90	46 786
Long first-degree university programmes[2]	15-24 year-olds; (1 045 897)	10.6	13	2 510
Short first-degree university programmes[3]	20-29 year-olds (1 263 040)	Negligibly small	30	37 891
Non-university tertiary programmes[4]	20-29 year-olds (1 263 040)	18.7	25	7 957
Continuing education and training[5]	workforce (3 828 200)	25.8*	40	543 600

* Participation rate.
1. Bevölkerungsstatistik (1995), Microcensus (1996), calculations by the study authors.
2. Microcensus Jahresergebnisse (1996), Bevölkerungsstatistik (1995), calculations by the study authors.
3. Bevölkerungsstatistik (1995), calculations by the study authors.
4. Microcensus (1996), Bevölkerungsstatistik (1995), calculations by the study authors.
5. Microcensus (1996), calculations by the study authors (Country report of Austria, Table 2.6).

Table A2.2. **Czech Republic – All educational sectors**
(data for late 1990s)

Level/Sector	Participants in 2005	Present participation rate	Participation gap (persons)
Secondary	115 000	67	68 000
Tertiary	127 000	10	211 000
Basic literacy programmes	20 000	5	43 000
Retraining programmes	158 000	5	468 000
Job-related education	2 000 000	30	1 753 000

Source: *Historical Yearbook of Education*, Institute for Information on Education, Prague (1998); *Statistical Yearbook of the Czech Republic* (1998); Czech Bureau of Statistics/Scientia, Prague (1998).

© OECD 2000

Table A2.3. **Finland – All educational sectors (policy targets)**
(data for late 1990s)

Sectors	Targets
Pre-school	Aim is to offer one year of pre-school for all children before compulsory education. 38 000 presently enrolled.
Comprehensive secondary	Maintain participation rates, and increase rate of transfer into upper secondary education to 100%.
Upper secondary vocational	Extend to three years, with minimum six months on-the-job learning; raise apprentices to 20% of vocational education enrolments.
Post-secondary education technical/vocational (non-university sector)	Polytechnics (AMK) and universities combined will enrol 60-65% of comprehensive secondary completers; increase places by 9 000 a year between 1996 and 1998; increase places in information technology sectors by 2 400 students per year, shared between polytechnics and universities.
Post-secondary education (university sector)	Expand graduate school enrolments by 250 places between 1997 and 1999; expand under-graduate enrolments in mathematics, natural sciences and technical sciences by 1 150 places; between 1998 and 2002, provide conversion education for 11 000 students; increase places in information technology sectors by 2 400 students per year, shared between polytechnics and universities.
Adults	Raise enrolments in adult education leading to qualifications from 26 500 in 1993/94 to 36 700 in 2000; ensure that there are an additional 35 000 (more if the employment situation warrants) student work years of continuing and complementary education; increase enrolments by 9 000 a year from 1997-2000, then scale back. Raise enrolments in vocational education for labour market programmes by 15 000 between 1996 and 1998. Increase for the over-50s their relative share of all enrolments.

Source: Council of State (1995), "Development plan for the period 1995-2000"; Committee for Lifelong Learning (1997), "Report to the Minister of Education and Science"; Ministry of Education; Statistics Finland.

Table A2.4. **Hungary – All educational sectors**
(data for late 1990s)

Level (population served)	Number in population (thousands)	Population served (thousands)	Proportion served	Suggested OECD targets (percentage served)	Participation gap (thousands)
ISCED 3 (0-18 year-olds)	2 535	1 938	76.4	90	344
ISCED 5 (19-30 year-olds)	1 748	0	0	30	524
ISCED 6 (19-30 year-olds)	1 748	241	13.8	13	0
ISCED 0-2 (15 year-old and older unqualified adults)	4 411	10	0.23	20	872
Unemployed	220	71	32.3	100	148
Employed	4 045	150	3.7	40	1 468

Source: Ministry of Education; Ministry of Labour; National Job Methodology Centre.

Annex 2

Table A2.5. **Japan – All educational sectors**
(data for late 1990s)

Sectors	Population (number)	Percentage served	Target (percentage)	Participation gap (number)
Foundation[1]	4 580 000	98	97	0
Tertiary[2]	3 250 000	69	60	0
Job-related training	n.a.	n.a.	n.a.	n.a.
Other adults[3]	40 930 000	48	65	10 700 000

n.a. Not available.
1. The population served at the foundation level includes enrolment (full-time/part-time) in high schools, correspondence courses and special training schools (upper secondary courses). The percentage served indicate the advancement rate to those schools and courses in 1996.
2. The population served at the tertiary education includes those enrolled in universities, junior colleges, colleges of technology and special training schools (tertiary education courses). The percentage served indicate the advancement rate to those institutes in 1996.
3. The population served includes enrolment in hobby/leisure education, excluding 410 000 enrolled in public skill development facilities.

Sources: Ministry of Education, Science, Sports and Culture (MESSC), "School Basic Survey, Report for 1996"; Ministry of Labour (1995), "Survey on Private-Sector Education and Training"; MESSC (1996), "Japan's Education Policy for 1996"; MESSC (1996), "Survey Concerning the Increasing Sophistication of Learning Needs and New Priorities"; NHK Broadcasting Culture Research Institute's Survey (1993); "Japanese Learning, 1993: Investigating Adult Attitudes and Behaviour"; MESSC, "Survey on Local Governments' Education Expenditure for 1995"; Country report for Japan, Table 2.6.

Table A2.6. **Korea – All educational sectors**
(data for late 1990s)

Sectors	Population (number)	Percentage served	Target (percentage)	Participation gap (number)
Foundation	747 849	38.9	40	8 226
Tertiary	799 897	33.9	45	88 788
Adult retraining for unemployed	419 000	21.4	50	119 834
Adult job-related training	20 377 000	0.7	10	1 895 061

Note: In the case of retraining for unemployed and job-related training, the participation data are limited to those of government-run training programmes; thus, the figures presented are substantially underestimated.
Sources: Bureau of Statistics (1995), "Household Census"; Ministry of Education (1995), "Statistics Indicators of Education"; Ministry of Labour (1997), "Statutes in Vocational Training".

© OECD 2000

Where are the Resources for Lifelong Learning?

Table A2.7. **Netherlands – Secondary education**
(data for late 1990s)

Educational levels below upper secondary	Percentage of population aged 27[1]	Population aged 27 at these levels	Target (reduction to)	Gap
Basic education	7.46	19 160	11 500	7 660
First level general secondary education (MAVO)	6.22	15 970	2 800	13 170
Junior vocational education (VBO)	12.67	32 530	11 400	21 130
Total	26.35[2]	67 660	25 700[3]	41 960

1. Total population aged 27 is 256 883 in 1996.
2. This is an overestimation of the number below upper secondary education, because these figures include some who have attained an apprenticeship diploma. However, more exact figures excluding all those with apprenticeship training do not exist.
3. 10% of total population aged 27.
Sources: Statistics Netherlands, *Monthly Statistics of the Population*, 1996/8; CBS (1993); and data on request by the sector Population (CBS).

Table A2.8. **Netherlands – Tertiary education**
(data for late 1990s)

Alternative target (%)	Population (number)	Percentage with diploma	Completion gap (number)
30	264 065	25	13 200
25	264 065	25	0

Note: Second column shows size cohort 30-year-olds at 1 January 1996. Fourth column shows the actual gap; to fill 5% gap between 25% and 30% you need 19 550 first year students (13 150 in HBO and 6 400 in WO).
Source: CBS (1997), *Deelnemers volwasseneneducatie* (Participants in Adult Education); and data provided on request by the sector Population (CBS).

Table A2.9. **Netherlands – Adult education and training**
(data for late 1990s)

Sectors	Population (in thousands)	Percentage served	Target (percentage)	Population gap
Adult education for poorly qualified (below ISCED 3)				
Not in the labour force (25-44)	513	11.5	20	(43 600)
			30	94 900
Not in the labour force (45-64)	1 051	4.3	20	(165 000)
			10	59 900
Long-term unemployed[1]				
All long-term unemployed	221	27.0	100	(162 000)
			50	51 000
of which lower educated	102	13.0	50	38 000
others	119	39.0	50	13 000
Job-related training				
Job-related training (25-64) below ISCED 3	1 481	20.8	40	(284 400)
			30	136 300
Other employees (at or above ISCED 3) following job-related training (25-64)	(3 922)	(39.0)	40	(39 200)

Note: Figures in brackets correspond to OECD targets referred to in Annex 1. Other figures correspond to alternative targets.
1. On the basis of the Statistics Netherlands definition of unemployed. If the definition "registered unemployed" would have been used, the number of long-term unemployed would have been lower and participation higher. Therefore the gaps would be lower, too.
Sources: CBS (1997), E*nquête beroepsbevolking* 1996 (Labour Force Survey 1996); SDU, The Hague; Janssen (1997), "Minder deelnemers basiseducatie, vavo en deeltijd-mbo" (Less participants in basic literacy, adult general secondary education and part-time vocational secondary education) in CBS, K*wartaalschrift Onder-wijsstatistieken*, 1997-II, p. 39; and data provided on request, OECD (1995).

Table A2.10. **Norway – All educational sectors (policy targets)**
(data for late 1990s)

Sectors	Targets
Foundation learning	All young people should complete upper secondary education and training with qualifications leading to either university entrance qualifications, a trade or journeyman's certificate or other vocational qualifications; particular focus needed on 18 year-olds who leave early to work.
Higher education	Aim for 50% of upper secondary completers to enter university; present capacity should be sufficient, but qualitative changes are needed in mix, to facilitate flow through university, and increase flexibility of institutions.
Adults: labour market training	Between 1994 and 1997, a 33% decline in unemployment was associated with a 52% decline in ordinary unemployed persons in training. Education and training for vocationally disabled is kept stable, or slightly increased. In the current tight labour market, the main emphasis is on advice, guidance, and job placements; in training, the emphasis is on on-the-job training and short vocational courses, except groups with a weak position in the labour market (long term unemployed, immigrants, single parents, etc. and the vocationally disabled).
Adults: basic language training	Presently, all non-Norwegian-speaking people should be provided with training up to the level where they are able to obtain work or participate in upper secondary education; participation is good. The amount of training provided depends to a great degree on the ability of the individual; those who are illiterate in their mother tongue may receive basic language training spread over several years. System under review; but it is expected that there is sufficient capacity to meet the increase in demand and scope that will result from any agreed change.
Adults: primary and secondary education for adults	Though nearly one million adults have not completed upper secondary education, fewer than 5 000 participate in primary and secondary education provided by municipalities. Government proposes that provision be expanded, though it is not clear by how much or where. Enrolment in municipal programmes has declined in recent years, while the number of adults taking the trade certificate has increased significantly (from around 7 000 in 1995 to almost 25 000 today). There is also an increase in the number of adults who themselves pay for most of their upper secondary education through the study associations (*studieforbund*) or different private providers.
Adults: job-related training	This is primarily the responsibility of the employers. Social partners have prepared the ground for a significant increase in the emphasis on continuing education and training for employees. Government proposes to support such an emphasis through better management of the supply of education and training to meet the needs of the working community, the use of information technology and distance education, and the documentation of the real competencies of adults, etc.

Sources: Statistics Norway; Ministry of Education, Research and Church Affairs; Directorate of Labour.

Table A2.11. **Sweden – All educational sectors (policy targets)**
(data for late 1990s)

Sectors	Targets
Upper secondary education	No specific targets set. In 1997, 87% of all 20 year-olds completed upper secondary; taking account of the number of 20-22 year-olds in municipal adult education and folk high school to acquire upper secondary competence, current policy mix is satisfactory.
Higher education	Participation in higher education is not particularly high, compared to other countries. Possible objective (though not officially endorsed) would be to: increase the proportion of 25 year-olds who have completed some course work in higher education, from 28% in 1997, to 35% by 2005; raise the proportion of 35 year-olds with at least three years of higher education, from 13% in 1997, to 15% in 2005; raise proportion of 25-54 year-olds who have completed some higher education from 28.5% in 1997 to 30% in 2005.
Adults: education	All adults should have the opportunity to acquire the next higher level of qualification; create 100 000 new places in adult education, plus 10 000 more in folk high school education, 5 000 more in municipal adult education at the compulsory level, and 5 000 places for advanced vocational training.
Adults: labour market training	Provide 20 000 places for vocationally oriented training; invest, in co-operation with IT companies, IT training for unemployed.
Adults: in-service and job-related training	Try to increase participation of those who do not presently take part in in-service and job-related training.

Sources: Statistics Sweden, SCB, *In-service training statistics 1987-1996*; *Labour force survey supplement*, LFS; *In-service training statistics June 1996*, LFS; *Register on Enrolment in Education 1995*; Folk high school 1995/96 Conscription Board; The National Agency for Education; Ministry of Education and Science; Council for Popular Adult Education; Swedish Labour Market Board.

Annex 3
Estimated Costs of Closing Participation Gaps

Table A3.1. **Austria – Estimated annual public costs (in ATS)**
(data for mid-1990s)

Education sector	Expenditure for closing the graduation and participation gaps – method a (in millions)	Expenditure for closing the graduation and participation gaps – method b (in millions)	Mean value (in millions)	Costs as a percentage of GDP
Upper secondary	3 350	4 531	3 940	0.2
Tertiary sector				
University – long forms	3 289	3 308	3 300	0.1
University – short forms	6 434	–	6 430	0.3
Non-university forms	1 351	1 867	1 610	0.1
Further vocational training	n.a.	15 241	15 240	0.6
Total			30 520	1.2

n.a. not available.
Method a: additional costs are calculated on the basis of the future age groups in population statistics. The disadvantage here is that repeaters and drop-outs are not taken into account, which leads to an underestimation of the expenditure necessary for closing the gaps.
Method b: additional costs are calculated on the basis of the rates of increase of the percentages of graduates. The disadvantage here is that the sizes of coming age groups are not considered, which leads to an overestimation of the expenditure necessary for closing the gaps insofar as the coming age groups are smaller than the current and older ones.
Sources: Bevölkerungsstatistik (1995); Microcensus (1996), calculations by the study authors; Microcensus jahresergebnisse (1996), Bevölkerungsstatistik (1995), calculations by the study authors; Bevölkerungsstatistik (1995), calculations by the study authors; Microcensus (1996), Bevölkerungsstatistik (1995), calculations by the study authors; Microcensus (1996), calculations by the study authors.

© OECD 2000

Table A3.2. **Czech Republic – Estimated annual public costs (in CZK)**
(data for mid-1990s)

Sector of education	Participation gap (persons)	Unit costs	Gap closing costs (in millions)	Costs as a percentage of GDP (1997)
Secondary	68 000	35 000	2 380	0.1
Tertiary	211 000	45 000	9 495	0.6
Basic literacy programmes	43 000	28 000	1 204	0.1
Retraining programmes	468 000	8 000	3 744	0.2
Job-related education	1 753 000	5 000	8 765	0.5
Total			25 588	1.6

Source: Institute for Information on Education (1998), *Historical Yearbook of Education*, Prague; *Statistical Yearbook of the Czech Republic* (1998); Czech Bureau of Statistics/Scientia, Prague (1998).

Table A3.3. **Finland – Estimated annual costs (in FIM)**
(and off-setting savings indicated by +)
(data for late 1990s)

	Political policy documents	Proposals of the Committee for Lifelong Learning	Costs as a percentage of GDP (1997)
Pre-school education	– 362 million	n.a.	0.1
Extending secondary level education	– 400 million, in addition probably costs of student financial aid	n.a.	0.1
Extending apprenticeship training	+ 35 million (student financial aid)	n.a.	+<0.1
Offering a place at an AMK institution or university to 60-65% of an age group	– 50 million (student financial aid)	n.a.	<0.1
Raising the level of skills and knowledge of adults with a weak educational background	n.a.	– 945 million (education) – 720 million (student financial aid)	0.2 0.1
Reserve for personnel training	n.a.	– 440 million (tax revenue transferred to later years)	0.1
Increased training for teachers and trainers	n.a.	– 20 million	<0.1
Resources becoming available after the temporary increase in educational provision	+ 686 million	n.a.	+0.1
Developing student financial aid as motivation to study	– 585 million	– 240 million	up to 0.1
Increasing education in the information sector	– 200 million	n.a.	<0.1
Total	c. – 0.9 billion	c. – 2.4 billion	0.1-0.4 depending on source of estimate

n.a. not available.
c = circa.
Source: Ministry of Education; Statistics Finland.

Table A3.4a. **Hungary – Estimated annual public costs (in HUF)**
(data for 1995)

Sector	Participation gap (thousands)	Unit costs (per person in thousands[1])	Costs of closing participation gap (in billions)	Costs as a share of GDP[2]
Foundation learning (kindergarten, primary and secondary education[3])	344	126	43	0.8
Higher education Short higher education programmes[4]	524	210	110	2.0
Training for unskilled adults[5]	872	39	34	0.6
Training for the unemployed[6]	148	130	19	0.4
Training for the employed[7]	1 468	66	97	1.8
Total			304	5.5

1. Average public cost in each sector in 1995 and in the 1995/96 school year.
2. GDP in 1995 amounted to HUF 5 530 billion.
3. Per student public cost of full-time education in kindergarten, primary and secondary school in the 1995/96 school year was between HUF 117 000 and 137 000 per person; costs are weighted by enrolment rate here.
4. Per student public cost in higher education in 1995/96 was HUF 420 000 per person per year (rounded). When calculating short higher education programmes 50% of this amount was used.
5. Per student public cost in employees' primary school is applied here.
6. The training cost weighted by enrolment rate for an unemployed in 1996 – according to OFA payments – was HUF 83 000. In addition to training costs, 97.5% of the unemployed received income supplement benefit, the per capita national average of which was HUF 47 000. Thus, total per capita training cost was HUF 130 000.
7. In 1995, in the active population 29% were unqualified, 28% were apprenticeship school graduates, 30% completed secondary education, and 13% completed higher education. As training costs of the unqualified, the costs of training for the unemployed (without the income supplement) in 1996 were taken into consideration, *i.e.* HUF 83 000. In workers' secondary schools per capita state support amounted to HUF 45 900 in 1996 – this sum was taken to calculate the specific further training costs of apprenticeship school graduates. Labour market training for the employed in 1996 was, in average, HUF 37 000 per capita. This sum was considered as state expenditure on training for secondary graduate labour force. In state financed part-time higher education per capita state expenditure was HUF 141 000, this taken as further training cost for higher education graduates. The weighted mean of these costs was HUF 66 400 per capita/year.

Source: Ministry of Education; Ministry of Labour; National Job Methodology Centre.

Table A3.4b. **Hungary – Estimated annual private costs (in HUF)**
(data for 1995)

	Costs to participants			Costs to employers		Participation gap (in thousands of people)	Costs of closing participation gap (billion HUF)	Costs as a percentage of GDP
Sector	Direct private cost (tuition fee, books and appliances) (HUF 1 000 per person)	Indirect private cost (transport) (HUF 1 000 per person)	Other indirect private cost (foregone earnings) (HUF 1 000 per person[1])	Direct private cost (foregone output, substitution[2]) (HUF 1 000 per person)				
Foundation learning (kindergarten, primary and secondary education[3])	10	114	n.a.	n.a.	344.1	42.7	0.8
Higher education[4]	40	182	337	n.a.	524.6	293.3	5.3
Training for unskilled adults[5]	10	30	11[6]	87[6]	872.2	59.7	1.1
Retraining for the unemployed	10	30	n.a.	n.a.	148.8	6.0	0.1
Training for the employed[7]	60	50	14	117	1 468.1	353.8	6.4
Total						755.4	13.7

n.a. not available.
1. Net average pays were calculated as HUF 21 000 per person per month for manual workers, and 26 000 for net national average (annual calculations include 13 months).
2. Employers' private costs were calculated with the method described above: manual workers' annual average pay plus contributions in 1995 was adopted for unskilled adults, and the average of mean annual pay and contributions of all employees in 1995 were applied for qualified adults.
3. In the foundation learning sector textbook costs were regarded as direct private cost (estimated average sum is HUF 10 000 per person per year). Other direct costs include a monthly average HUF 1 000 as transportation cost. In addition, one-third of the annual average net pay (HUF 8 500 per person per month) is calculated for living/child care cost.
4. In case of higher education, an average HUF 3 000 per month tuition fee (for 10 month), and HUF 40 000 per year textbook cost was determined. Foregone earning was equal to the average annual net pay of all employees in 1995, transportation cost was HUF 2 000 per person per month, and the accommodation (in dormitory) cost on the average was HUF 6 000 per person per month (the latter two are calculated for 10 months). In addition, one-third of the annual average net pay (HUF 8 500 per person per month) is calculated for living cost (for 12 months).
5. In case of unskilled adult training full tuition fee exemption was assumed along with only HUF 10 000 per person as textbook, educational appliances and tuition fee cost. Foregone earning was determined as 4% of manual workers' annual net average pay in 1995, while the average transportation cost was HUF 3 000 per month (for 10 months).
6. Out of the 4 411 thousand poorly qualified population only 1 283 thousand, i.e. 29% were economically active in 1995. Lost production and foregone earning was, therefore, calculated only for 29% of the participation gap.
7. As for the qualified population – taking state support into account – tuition fee was calculated to be HUF 30 000 per year on the average, another HUF 30 000 for textbooks and educational appliances, and HUF 5 000 per month for transportation cost (for 10 months). Foregone earning was determined as 20% of the annual net average pay of all those employed in 1995.

Source: Ministry of Education; Ministry of Labour; National Job Methodology Centre.

Annex 3

Table A3.5. **Japan – Estimated annual public costs (in JPY)**
(data for 1994)

Sectors	Participation gap (number)	Unit costs	Costs of closing the gap	Costs as a percentage of GDP
Foundation[1]	0	2 069 000	0	0
Tertiary[2]	0	2 282 000	0	0
Adult (poorly qualified)	n.a.	n.a.	n.a.	n.a.
Basic literacy	0	0	0	0
Retraining for unemployed	n.a.	n.a.	n.a.	n.a.
Job-related training	n.a.	n.a.	n.a.	n.a.
Other adults	10 700 000	330 000	3 536 (billion)	0.7
Total				0.7

n.a. not available.
1. Unit costs of foundation are those of full-time high schools. The percentage of current public expenditures is an estimation drawn from some prefectural governments' practices.
2. Unit costs of tertiary education are those of 4-year universities. The percentage of current public expenditures is the result of several surveys.
Source: Ministry of Education, Science, Sports and Culture (MESSC), "School Basic Survey, Report for 1996"; Ministry of Labour (1995), "Survey on Private-Sector Education and Training"; MESSC (1996), "Japan's Education Policy for 1996"; MESSC (1996), "Survey Concerning the Increasing Sophistication of Learning Needs and New Priorities"; NHK Broadcasting Culture Research Institute's 1993 survey (1996), "Japanese Learning, 1993: Investigating Adult Attitudes and Behaviour"; MESSC, "Survey on Local Governments' Education Expenditure for 1995".

Table A3.6. **Korea – Estimated annual public costs (in KRW)**
(data for 1995)

Sectors	Participation gap (number)	Unit costs	Cost of closing the gap (in thousands)	Costs as a percentage of GDP
Foundation	8 226	1 785 300	14 685 877.8	<0.1
Tertiary	88 788	4 227 300 (University)	375 333 512.4	0.1
Adult (poorly qualified)	n.a.	n.a.	n.a.	n.a.
Retraining for unemployed	119 834	n.a.	n.a.	
Job-related training	1 895 06	n.a.	n.a.	
Total			390 019 390.2	0.1

n.a. not available.
Source: Bureau of Statistics (1995), "Household Census"; Ministry of Education (1995), "Statistics Indicators of Education"; Ministry of Labour (1997), "Statutes in Vocational Training"; Ministry of Education (1996), "Statistical Yearbook of Education"; Ministry of Labour (1995), "Details of the Budget".

© OECD 2000

Table A3.7a. **Netherlands – Estimated annual public costs of closing the participation gap in secondary education (in NLG)**
(data for mid-1990s)

Current educational level	Participation gap	Educational paths - Number of students	Educational paths - Specific path in years	Unit costs	Unit costs contribution study costs/ study grants	Total costs (in millions)
Basic education	7 660	3 830	3 years of VBO + 3 years of apprenticeship	39 000	3 200	161.6
		3 830	3 years of VBO + 4 years of apprenticeship	43 000	3 200	177.0
First level general secondary education (MAVO)	13 170	5 270	3 years of MBO	26 400	17 400	230.8
		7 900	4 years of MBO	35 200	23 200	461.4
Junior vocational education (VBO)	21 130	10 570	3 years of apprenticeship	12 000	–	126.8
		10 560	4 years of apprenticeship	16 000	–	169.0
Total	41 960					1 326.6

Source: CBS (1997), Deelnemers volwasseneneducatie (Participants in Adult Education); data provided on request by the sector Population (CBS); Statistics Netherlands, Monthly Statistics of the Population, 1996/8; CBS, 1993; OCW (1997), Financial key data on education; OCW, The education budget 1995, 1997; country report on the Netherlands, Table 2.7a.

Table A3.7b. **Netherlands – Estimated annual public costs of closing the completion gap in upper secondary and higher education[1] (in NLG)**
(data for mid-1990s)

Sectors	Participation gap	Unit costs	Cost of closing the gap (in billions)	As a percentage of current public expenditure (%)
Upper secondary education	41 960	Weighted calculations[2]	1.33	0.70
Higher education	13 200 (target 30%)	Weighted calculations[3]	1.19	0.63
Higher education	0 (target 25%)	Weighted calculations[3]	0	0

1. This is a slight underestimation because the costs of closing the gap refer to previous years and are not corrected for inflation.
2. See country report, Table 2.7a.
3. See country report, Chapter 2, Annex Table A.3.

Sources: CBS (1997), Deelnemers volwasseneneducatie (Participants in Adult Education); data provided on request by the sector Population (CBS); Statistics Netherlands, Monthly Statistics of the Population, 1996/8; CBS (1993); OCW (1997), Financial key data on education; OCW, The education budget 1995, 1997.

Table A3.7c. **Netherlands – Estimated annual public costs of closing the enrolments gaps in the relevant types of adult education (in NLG)**
(data for mid-1990s)

Sectors	Target (%)	Participation gap (number)	Unit costs	Cost of closing the gap (in thousands)	As a percentage of current public expenditure[1]
Adult education for poorly qualified (below ISCED 3)					
Not in the labour force (25-44)	30 (20)	94 900 (43 600)	2 070	196 443 (90 252)	0.10 (0.05)
Not in the labour force (45-64)	10 (20)	59 900 (165 000)	2 070	123 993 (341 550)	0.07 (0.18)
All long-term unemployed	50 (100)	51 000 (162 000)	5 900	301 000 (956 000)	0.16 (0.50)
Job-related training					
Job-related training (below ISCED 3) (25-64)	30 (40)	136 300 (284 400)	1 413	192 592 (401 857)	0.10 (0.21)
Other adult employees (at or above ISCED 3) following job-related training (25-64)	(40)	(39 200)	(1 413)	(55 390)	(0.03)
Total		694 200		1 845 049	0.98
Total under alternative targets		381 300		869 418	0.46

Note: Figures in brackets correspond to OECD targets referred to in Annex 1; other figures correspond to alternative targets.
1. Current public expenditure budget for central government in 1998, minus outlays for debt relief.
Source: CBS (1997), Enquête beroepsbevolking 1996 (Labour Force Survey 1996), SDU, The Hague; Janssen (1997), "Minder deelnemers basiseducatie, vavo en deeltijd-mbo" (Less participants in basic literacy, adult general secondary education and part-time vocational secondary education), in CBS, Kwartaalschrift Onder-wijsstatistieken, 1997 II, p. 39; Country report on the Netherlands, Table 2.6c; Bronneman-Helmers (1992), Volwasseneneducatie tussen markt en overheid (Adult education between market and government), SCP, Rijs-wijk, p. 87; CBS (1995), Bedrijfsopleidingen 1993, particuliere sector (Employer Sponsored Training 1993, Private Sector), Voorburg/Heerlen, pp. 37-59; Koning, Zandvliet and Knol (1993), Kosten en Baten van het Centrum Vakopleiding, het CBB en de Vrouwenvakschool (Costs and benefits of the centre for vocational training, the CBB and the female vocational school), NEI, Rotterdam; Arbeidsvoorziening (1996), Jaarverslag 1996 (Annual Report 1996), Zoetermeer; Ministerie van Financiën (1997), Samenvatting miljoenennota 1998 (Summary Budget 1998) [Internet: http://www.minfin.nl.].

© OECD 2000

Table A3.7d. **Netherlands – Summary of public costs of closing the participation gap for all relevant sectors (in NLG)**
(data for mid-1990s)

Sector	Participation gap (number)	Total costs per year (in billions)	Costs as a percentage of GDP
Secondary education	41 960	1.33	0.2
Higher education	13 150	1.19	0.2
Adult education	694 200	1.85	0.3
Total	749 310	4.37	0.6

Source: See Tables A3.7a through A3.7c.

Table A3.8. **Norway – Estimated central government costs of meeting targets in all educational sectors**
(dates indicated where appropriate)

Sectors	Estimated costs
Foundation learning	n.a
Higher education	Sufficient capacity to achieve objectives; qualitative changes are expected to incur no additional costs
Adults: labour market training	No expansion expected
Adults: basic language training	Increased by NOK 60 million in 1998; more increases expected in future
Adults: primary and secondary education for adults	Increased resources expected to be needed, but no definite amounts yet (1998)
Adults: Job-related training	Minimal public costs

n.a. not available.
Source: Statistics Norway; Ministry of Education, Research and Church Affairs; Directorate of Labour.

Table A3.9. **Sweden – Estimated central government costs of meeting targets in all educational sectors**
(dates indicated where appropriate)

Sectors	Estimated costs
Upper secondary education	Targets being met; no additional cost
Higher education	Can be met with no additional resource
Adults: education	SEK 5 billion for 18 months 1997-1998 (0.2% of GDP)
Adults: labour market training	SEK 2 billion in 1998 (0.1% of GDP)
Adults: in-service and job-related training	Principally the responsibility of the social partners; possible resource implications for government, if any, are not yet available

Sources: Statistics Sweden, SCB, *In-service training statistics* 1987-1996; Labour force survey supplement, LFS; *In-service training statistics* (1996), LFS; *Register on Enrolment in Education* (1995); Folk high school 1995/96 Conscription Board; The National Agency for Education; Ministry of Education and Science; Council for Popular Adult Education; Swedish Labour Market Board; *Annual Statistical Yearbook* 1990-1994, "Primary Municipality Personnel 1996" (Statistical Messages AM 52 SM9701); AMS Annual Report 1995/96.

© OECD 2000

The following persons co-ordinated preparation of the country reports

Mr. Jorma Ahola, Ministry of Education Finland.
Ms. Marie Bucht, Ministry of Education and Science, Sweden.
Ms. Annelise Hauch, Ministry of Education, Denmark.
Mr. Chon-Sun Ihm, Korean Educational Development Institute, Korea.
Mr. Ernst Koller, Federal Ministry for Education and Cultural Affairs, Austria.
Ms. Jarmila Modra, National Training Fund, Czech Republic.
Mr. Lucio Pusci, Ministry of Education, Italy.
Mr. Yutaka Shiraishi, Kyoto University, Japan.
Mr. Peter Soltesz, Ministry of Culture and Education, Hungary.
Ms. Margrethe Steen Hernes, Ministry of Education, Research and Church Affairs, Norway.
Mr. Frans de Vijlder, Ministry of Education, Culture and Science, Netherlands.

© OECD 2000

OECD PUBLICATIONS, 2, rue André-Pascal, 75775 PARIS CEDEX 16
PRINTED IN FRANCE
(91 2000 03 1 P) ISBN 92-64-17677-2 – No. 51283 2000